Black Mothers
HOLD THE LINE
Collection, Vol. 1

Edited by Dominique J. Smiley

DEDICATION

To the 15 Queen authors who stepped out of their comfort zone, looked fear straight in the eye, and spoke their truth, I appreciate you! You mustered up the courage to allow your walls to come down and chains to be broken when you could have kept your story buried inside, and for this, I say thank you!

Thank you for revealing, releasing, and restoring your whole self so that your testimony can be another Queen's survival guide.

- Patricia D. Harris

CHAPTERS

INTRODUCTION
Patricia D. Harris

In war, "hold the line" means remaining steadfastly in position during combat. Little did I know in October 2017, God was preparing me for war. He provided me with a four-edge sword that would prove deadly to the enemy once I knew how to use it properly. This sword consisted of four actions I was to take when confronted by the enemy: **pause** and take a deep breath, **process** and put my mind at rest, **pray** knowing God would hear my cry, and then **proceed** in faith, thanking God for His mercy and grace. It took me three long years to even learn the value of this weapon and to apply it to my life.

On June 26, 2020, I was confronted with a challenge in my life that I would quickly understand was the war God was preparing me for. For some time, I felt something was approaching; something I was really hoping to avoid, but realized after all hell broke loose, I was not in the right position to avoid it. While a part of me somewhat understood what was happening, I was still finding it difficult to understand the totality of it all. As I began this new chapter of my life, some called it a moment, but for several months, it felt more like a tsunami. I felt a disconnect, a pulling away of all that I loved and just like in a tsunami, in one full gush, everything came crashing down on me. Through many nights of crying myself to sleep, beating myself up, questioning my self-worth and yes, even getting upset with God, I realized this was so much bigger than myself. This moment of interruption was meant to prepare me for what was to come and how God planned on using me.

In order to be used, there were some things I needed to *reveal, release* and to *restore* concerning myself; those things inside of me that were holding me captive, that were preventing me from seeing myself the way God saw me; those things that kept me on the run, that made me want to flee time and time again; those things that kept me looking in the past, preventing me from living in the present, in God's presence, and anticipating the future with great hope. As those things surfaced, it became clearer just how out of position I was. I was reminded of different times I didn't show up the way I should have, times I didn't show compassion or provide understanding on any level, all because of my inner turmoil, the baggage I continued to carry around and hold on to as if it were a trophy I won. All those times, I should have sought God's help instead of leaning on my own understanding.

As months passed and I drew closer to God, on October 20, 2020, my assignment became clear: **hold the line, don't move, and don't retreat!** Put on the full armor, stand your ground, remain steady and don't react. The weight of this revelation came at me again like the wave from a tsunami, but this time I embraced it with open arms. I realized because of what I refused to *reveal, release,* and *restore,* I stayed on the run, trying to escape my fear of rejection, not being valued, or not being understood or loved.

I didn't realize that all the times I left my post, I left my husband, my children, and my grandchildren unprotected. Wow, what an eye opener and an honor; an honor that God loved me enough to give me a second chance, and even before I knew what was really going on, he was preparing me. Even though I still make mistakes, I yearn for what God has for me. The desire to sit in His presence consumed me, and I created a place where I could go and just bask in His glory. The desire to please Him, to hear Him say, "I see you, I see your efforts and I am pleased," brings me great joy. I started taking my eyes off myself and my current situation and started wholeheartedly trusting what God was placing in my spirit. I began rebuking whatever didn't line up with God's word, and the process of doing things differently than what I did in the past took root. See, I now know the role I play as a woman, a wife, a mother, a daughter, a sister, an aunt, a grandmother, and a friend. There is a responsibility that I have and every time I leave my post, every time I run out of fear and disappointment, I leave those that I love unprotected.

By "holding the line," *I can strategize with the greatest general of all.*

By holding the line, *I can see how I got tripped up and let the enemy infiltrate the camp.*

By holding the line, *I can admit I got fearful and wanted to run, but I paused, processed, prayed, and proceeded back on to the battlefield.*

I am excited to share the real-life testimonies of 15 other queen authors who have also accepted their role on the battlefield of life and who are holding the line despite the enemy's tactics on behalf of those that they truly love!

Queens, we may have lost many battles, but we will not lose the war. There are some things that we as women were only called to do, but we must be in position.

WE MUST HOLD THE LINE!

Dear Diary:

"Revelation…I have to acknowledge who I am in God. You created me, You saved me, You called me, and You chose me. It is time I start walking in it!"

A POEM FROM MY HEART, FROM A SEASON IN MY LIFE
AMK Purnell

My mommy and daddy never told me there would be days like this
> when my innocence would be taken from me.
Afraid to tell mommy and daddy,
so I keep the pain hidden inside for years to come.
For once in my life I am free
about to embark on a life of my own;
I would not be alone, and I was getting married.
After the marriage came two beautiful boys,
but I was still lost, searching for something.
I felt empty inside carrying around this heavy secret.
I was still trying to find my *own* identity.
My goal was to bury it deep down inside my heart and soul.
I didn't know who I was because I was so damaged inside.
For years I pretended to be someone else.
Finally realizing that's not me
Life goes on without you.
I am at a crossroads
One of the frightening crossroads was the loss of my Dad.
I was not able to tell him my secret of pain.
Then came more hardship and pain.
A road where there are two directions; at this point should I tell my
> Mom or husband?

Which road do I take?

I decide to tell my husband, but he must not tell anyone.

There would be too much pain in the family

but shortly after, my husband and I divorce.

Then came more pain and agony.

Can someone help me on this path?

You don't know how badly I wanted to tell my best friend, my
    mother.

But I could not allow her to endure any more pain.

Yet, I kept going, day by day, waiting, searching, and feeling.

Then after years of me carrying the secret around, my Mom passed
    away.

She will not know my painful secret.

Then came more deep agony and pain.

I felt even more lost without my Mom

but one day, as I cried and prayed out to God,

He whispered, "*I got you, and I love you.*"

He said, "*Let the rivers flow, let it go. I am with you.*"

After that great revelation, a friend suggested talking to a counselor.

I was apprehensive, but there was a great nudging in my spirit.

Then on one particularly rainy day, I decided to go to counseling.

The rain reminded me of God telling me to let my tears flow.

For me, this was part of my healing process.

After constant prayer and counseling, I felt like I was no longer
    broken.

I could finally say I was on the right road to healing.

Finally, after years of hoping, my day came, and I knew where I
    belonged.

So every day after my marvelous revelations from God and a close
    friend,

I knew I was where I was supposed to be the entire time on my
    crossroad.

My crossroad was there to make me a strong godly mother, wife,
    sister, and friend for a divine purpose.

So, at my crossroad, I realized I had to keep pushing through the
pain life will bring.

Until my end, I keep living like mommy and daddy would want me
to do.

Crossroads are only stepping stones to a blessed future ordained by
God.

The End

About *AMK Purnell*

At this season in her life, Purnell considers herself a woman of Godly wisdom. There have been many ups and downs, but God sustained her. God blessed her with two handsome young men, a four-year-old grandson, the ability to retire from law enforcement after 29 years, and a happy marriage to a supportive, loving man. She received her undergraduate degree in Psychology and recently her Master's in Clinical Mental Health. Her plan for this season in her life is to assist others in their journey and let them know God will be with them every step of the way.

Dear Diary:

"And God further said..."

WE RISE ABOVE
Charlotte Miller-Lacy

It's amazing how a word, certain sound, location, music or event can bring you right back to an emotion you felt months or years ago. For instance, there is a commercial playing on the television for GEICO. The song has nothing to do with insurance but as soon as I hear "Whoomp! There It Is" by Tag Team, I go back to meeting the man of my dreams who is now my husband. We met at a block party in "West Philadelphia born and raised." Yes, I had to use that one from Will Smith, the Fresh Prince. Both of us were just coming out of "broken relationships" with children, boys to be exact. That's how we met at the block party—our boys got into a fight over a ball.

Twenty-eight years later, we have five grown men between us, one bonus daughter I picked, seven granddaughters and two grandsons. I laugh about it and the heat I gave my husband when we fell in love and decided to blend two families from broken relationships into one.

We dated and found out we had similar interests, values, and morals. On one of our dates, he invited me to a block party (yes, they are big in the summertime in Philadelphia). It was on his parents' block and they were having family and friends over. Our children were with our exes, so it was just me and him attending. This block party was one of the big events of the neighborhood. Everyone and anyone was there. I met his parents and immediately fell in love with them. They were the social butterflies of the community and everyone knew them and loved them.

While in the kitchen meeting his family and talking with his mother, she said "I heard you have children."

I said, "Yes, two boys." She asked why I didn't bring them with me, and I told her they were with their dad.

She looked at me and said, "Oh ok. I just want you to know your kids are always a package deal in relationships and are welcome here whenever you want to bring them." I knew right then he came from a "good stock," as they say.

I was the custodial parent and my ex had visitation. The same played out for my husband. Of course, we talked about how things went wrong in each relationship, but our conversations were more about how we were feeling about each other. Yes, we were feeling each other physically and emotionally and were moving full speed ahead. We decided to start doing family things together, especially when he had his sons. We got engaged, moved in together, and started planning a life together. I knew and understood that my husband's children were going to have to have access to him, I just didn't realize what type of access the ex was going to need!

I remember my pastor talking about when we start dating people, for some reason we don't ask the hard questions early. We figured the boys would be okay because they were kids and they had already started hanging out with each other doing brotherly things and getting along as best as boys would. Even though my husband's boys didn't live in the house with us, we didn't want them to feel like visitors. All the boys shared rooms with things that were personal to them; they had their own dressers, clothes, bed linens, pictures, games, and toys.

Remember, I am writing this from my perspective. On my side, my ex was respectful, timely, and cordial relating to my new relationship. On my husband's side, his ex was disrespectful, unaccommodating, and outright rude.

As I write this, I can still feel the emotions I felt the day the first incident between us happened. Just for some background, leading up to us getting married, my husband handled everything with his ex regarding his sons concerning their visits, support and so on.

It was a Saturday afternoon, and my "in-loves" were over for a barbecue. The house phone rang, and I answered it, never realizing that what would transpire would affect our household for a long time to come.

Oh no she didn't just call my house and say to me, "Put Dave on the phone!" (David is my husband). So of course, everything in me went from 0 to 1000 real quick (I was still a work in progress).

"Uhh, excuse you?! Let's back this up! We will not do this this way!"

She then said, "Get used to it, especially since my kids will be at your house. Can I speak with their father?!"

My reply was, "Yes, when you learn how to address me first," and I hung up! She kept calling right back. Finally, I told my husband, and he picked up the phone and proceeded to have a heated conversation with her. Blended family or blended baby mama drama?

From that day, it was on and popping. Remember, I really hadn't had any interactions with this woman before, everything went through my husband. So, I couldn't understand and wasn't trying to understand what was going on.

I wanted my husband to show his love and loyalty to me and our marriage and put her in her place, but he needed to do it how I said she needed to be put in her place!

I can't remember every little detail, but it went something like:

"You need to call her and tell her in front of me! She had better not call this house and disrespect your wife and our home! Tell her that you love me and not her. Get over it and move on!"

All about me, right? And remember, she only asked me to put Dave on the phone.

He wanted to know why all of that needed to be said. It needed to be said because it was going to make me feel better. The mere fact that he was questioning me was an issue. *Why are you questioning me? Why aren't you as mad, hot, and angry as I am?* This was truly an issue. The seeds of discord, mistrust, demand, and loud voices had been planted in our house!

At the time I didn't realize I was giving her authority over what was happening in our house and between my husband and I. Needless to say it caused a lot of hurt feelings, arguments, and ultimatums.

But it also speaks to the woman I thought I was until I was faced with a situation that required something else of me. It required me to rest, relax, and allow the man I married, who was also the father to children she had, to handle that situation as he had in the beginning. The man I married was very intentional in how he wanted his sons to see him as a man and father. That included how he treated their mother. No matter how she felt about their situation, he wanted his children to feel good about him and his concern for them.

When this situation happened, it went from bad to worse real fast! We had to go to court and weren't able to see the kids as much. There were verbal fights and arguments, suspicions, and accusations. At that time, I could not see that the man I was arguing with was the same man I shared similar interests, values, and morals with, but he was the same man I fell in love with because of how he handled himself and situations. I now needed to control situations because *she* made me feel crazy with emotions that were left over from past relationships—the need to control everything, mistrust, hurt feelings, and manipulation we as women know oh so well. The need to do that was hurting my family, marriage, home, and my feelings. I am a natural nurturer and I had allowed someone to cause my household to be out of harmony and control.

Little prayer, little power. Much prayer, much power was my first line of defense. I had to pray for my husband, marriage, family, home, myself, and everyone attached to this situation. Yes, that meant praying for her as well! The one thing I realized was I already had the power the day she called on the phone; I could have simply called my husband to the telephone and showed her she could come with whatever she wanted, but she couldn't bring me into her plan. I am sure down the line there would have been something else, but by doing that, I could have set the tone for any other confrontations.

My husband and I were able to talk about how to handle these types of situations going forward. And they did continue to happen for a few years until the boys were older. What changed were the reactions she didn't get from us. Relationships are built on several levels; one is **understanding**. I realized she was looking at her children sharing the life she wanted in another house with their dad. **Trust** is another one. *How do I get her to trust me?* One of the first things I did was start calling her to check on the boys. I would also ask her opinion on the boys' likes and dislikes as well as acknowledging her position as the custodial parent and the great job she was doing. I volunteered to be an emergency contact person at school or for extracurricular activities they were in. That actually worked out well. One of the boys got sick at school and neither his mother nor my husband could get to him in a timely manner. I was the one who picked him up from the nurse until his mother was able to come and get him. **Acceptance;** interactions like these allowed the both of us to see each other as nurturing mothers who only wanted the best for the children entrusted in our care. From that point, she would often reach out to me when the boys were in sporting events, plays, award ceremonies and graduations to make sure it was on our calendar, and we could attend and celebrate the boys' milestones together. **Appreciation;** we appreciated what each of us brought to the table for the boys; they had a mother and a mother figure who looked after them and cared about their wellbeing.

As a woman, wife, mother, and mother figure, I felt it was my responsibility to hold the line for my husband, our sons, our family, and our home. I had to take back my power as a wife, mother, and nurturer. I realized what I was fighting for and against and I was not willing to let the line holding our happy life together be broken!

About *Charlotte Miller-Lacy*

Charlotte and David live a happy and full life together. They enjoy spending time with family, especially all the grandkids. Being recognized and known as "Momma Lacy" in the community is something that is near and dear to Charlotte's heart. Charlotte has five principles that have framed her journey to success—*Faith, Family, Friends, Persistence, and a Positive Attitude!*

Dear Diary:

"Raising my level of confidence, doing something different and trusting in God…"

THE JOURNEY BACK TO ME
Dawn L. Pipkin

"My mission in life is not merely to survive, but to thrive; and to do so with some passion, some compassion, some humor, and some style."

- *Maya Angelou*

The mission in life quote by the amazing Dr. Maya Angelou is eye opening and is so relevant in this next chapter of my journey called life. It has given me confidence in my emerging passion for purpose and the understanding that the power of the tongue can demolish the very act of fear. This quote is truly influential because for years I was always the passive passenger riding in the vehicle of survival with fear as the driver. It was a dangerous vehicle filled with depression, anxiety, low self-esteem, abandonment, isolation, brokenness, and regret. This vehicle drove me to make many poor decisions that have affected my movement in time—decisions that left me mentally, physically, financially, emotionally, and spiritually broken to the point of low self-recognition. The vehicle of survival sure took me through some hills and valleys, but through it all I've learned significant lessons that shaped my thought pattern on how valuable I am as a Black woman but more so as a single Black mother.

Self-Identification

It was 12:30 p.m. on a Sunday morning in April 2020. I woke up feeling fatigued and physically heavy. It felt like someone took a huge boulder and dropped it on my body. It was the first time in years that I woke up past 8 a.m. on a Sunday. I slowly climbed out of bed, drank the bottle of water on my nightstand, and then I walked to the bathroom. Oddly, I was walking at a snail's pace. The bathroom was literally three steps across the hall, but I felt like I was walking ten miles. Once I made it to the bathroom, I brushed my teeth, washed my face, looked in the mirror and stared. I am not sure how long I was staring in the mirror, but it was long enough to know that I was not happy with who was staring back at me. I saw a Black woman who was lost. She appeared worn out and disheveled. She was at her wits' end about being unhealthy, stagnant, unenthusiastic, and unsatisfied.

I saw this Black woman before. It was ten years ago. She was the over 300-pound stressed out woman who wore the deceptive mask of "I'm ok." She was the low self-esteemed, given up on purpose, and feeling inadequate woman. She was the one who lost herself, or should I say, she never found herself. She was the woman trying to meet everyone else's needs and keep busy.

Staring at this lady was unbelievable. Here it was ten years later and for the life of me this perplexed Black woman found her way back into my life. I stared at her, heartbroken. Tears formed, but I did not allow them to fall because I had no more energy to deal with the emotional anguish. After collecting myself, I went into the living room and sat down on the couch. I thought about what COVID-19 revealed. It revealed that I never gave myself enough room to authentically discover myself. If there was one thing I knew, it was that I never wanted to see that Black woman again, and it was important for me to take the steps toward self-care. I pulled out my journal and started writing. I wrote what I did not like about myself, and I wrote about how I was going to change that personal perspective. It felt like I was writing for hours, but I was determined to change the narrative of my story. After writing, I went back to the mirror. I stood there with a look of "*Listen here!*" and informed the Black woman, "*You are getting up and staying up this time!*" It was that Sunday after staring in the mirror at myself when I began to make a permanent change.

Twenty twenty-one definitely became my year of self-identification. Yes, it took me 41 years and being in the middle of a deadly pandemic to realize what God has created, which is a beautiful, resilient, compassionate, and mighty masterpiece. I am uniquely crafted to grow and accomplish limitlessly.

Wait a minute! I just had a *Wow!* moment; I just got excited about the word *limitlessly*. The reason for my excitement is I worried about the thoughts and negative opinions of others to the point where I created my own fear to succeed. Some of the negative remarks were: "You can't do this," and "You aren't about nothing." I even had a loved one tell me that the family did not believe I belonged biologically. I had to have a conversation with my parents, and according to them, the statement was a lie, but talk about gut-punching blows to the mind and heart. It was very hurtful to hear. I allowed the rejections to play in my head, and I truly believed I could not do anything correctly. I doubted if I was good enough. I even focused too much on "I did not belong."

People do not take the time to think before speaking. If that were the case, then they would compassionately know that words alone can cause damage, and the damage caused me to lack self-identity. I hid behind the smiling mask and set limits that I did not believe I could achieve. Because of the fear of rejection, the limits I set depended on the level of enthusiasm I had about an idea or project. I had restricted myself when vocalizing my concerns with others fearing that I would not be heard. I even restricted myself on how much I should focus on my well-being, fearing that people would consider me selfish and thoughtless, so to know that I can limitlessly accomplish my goals is a breath of fresh air.

It is a wonderful feeling to have clarity on who you are and what you are destined to achieve. It is amazing to be mentally free from the bondage of other people's hostile words. I wholeheartedly believe those words were set up to devour me. John 10:10 (AMP) states, *"The thief comes only in order to steal and kill and destroy…."* Those who did not have my best interest at heart used words to kill my positive thoughts, to steal my joy and drive to pursue personal goals, and to destroy the vision God gave me. They wanted me to fail, but in my failures, I found my identity and freedom. I am free to be genuinely me. This change did not happen overnight. At first, it was a struggle. I would cry some days. I would overeat other days. I would not communicate with certain people many days. In between those hard days, I would go for walks with my mask on, of course. I would pull out my sewing machine and watch YouTube tutorials to make masks. I would video chat with my family. Laughing with them gave me so much joy, I would have to write a whole other story about the fun we had. Prayer was and continues to be vital.

Music really helped me too. I love all types of genres, so many times I would just dance and sing throughout my home. I even found myself doing Tik Toks with my daughter. Each day I made sure I was being productive in self-care and in doing so, I started to shed negativity. I am still progressing, but my new discovered freedom has opened my eyes to understand that there is so much more to life. It also helped me to take ownership of my own choices. This freedom has opened the door for the journey back to me.

Self-Ownership

Eight years ago, my daughter and I left Oxford, Pennsylvania, and we moved back to my home state, Delaware. We moved because of an unexpected loss of employment. Even though I was receiving unemployment benefits, it was a difficult period for me and my daughter. It was hard to manage my continuous household bills. It took seven months for me to obtain employment, and it was a no brainer that living near my job would be beneficial financially, so the move to Delaware was supposed to be a fresh start after facing hardship. Prior to the move, I raised my daughter in a predominately white and Hispanic environment. I thought the move was going to be great, especially because my daughter would finally be around children she could connect with culturally.

Well, I was so wrong. I saw my super happy 11-year-old girl change to a hard-hitting aggressive 11-year-old girl. She faced many challenges, and I saw the change as soon as she started her third week of middle school. Apparently, there was a seventh-grade girl who wanted to fight my daughter. According to my daughter, she did not know why this girl wanted to fight her, but every day this girl made it known that she did not like her.

One day, at the end of basketball practice, a group of the girls surrounded her inside of the locker room, blocking the only exit, and they made sure it was tightly sealed. It was impossible for my daughter to avoid the confrontation; she defended herself in that locker room, proving that the new sixth-grade girl was not weak. I pulled in the parking lot of the school and my daughter was marching out of the school with her chest poked out and hair out of place. She opened the door and got into the car. She sat quietly for a moment with this angry expression. I looked at her with concern, and before I could ask about practice, she told me that she had gotten into a fight. She explained all the details. I asked her if she was okay and if she had any injuries, but she reassured me that she handled her business, and she was not hurt. I allowed her to express her feelings. Once we reached the apartment, we sat down, and I prepared her for any repercussions she would face the next day of school. I did teach her that she has a right to protect herself, so I was not upset with my daughter for standing up for herself on that day.

After that third week, I noticed that she was in a fight every week. She had to prove that she was not the one to bully. Every day, she had to prepare herself for altercations with different female and male students. Each one of those students were sent by the girl because she knew it was hard to win on her own. I spent more time at the school than I did at work. Each day at the middle school, I could see her losing a piece of herself.

Similar to me, she created a mask to hide any hurt or pain. The more she hid behind the mask, the more I became angry and closed-minded to her experience. I expected her to ignore the problem and move forward without entertaining the shenanigans. I became frustrated while she was facing trauma. My daughter dealt with these problems her entire time of middle school. Once she entered high school, the problems with the same girl were sure to continue, but I made it up in my mind that the fighting had to stop, so I met with the administration to find a solution. It took some time, but I realized that I had to change my perspective on what my daughter was going through. It took an awesome family organization in Wilmington, Delaware during her freshman year of high school to help me be accountable as a mother. This organization helped me own my faults in not being compassionate to her everyday experiences. I now comprehend the significance of self-ownership.

Whew! Owning my stuff was a difficult pill to swallow, but now I can laugh about my stubbornness. There was a time that I refused to be vulnerable. I did not want to believe that I, too, fell short in teaching my daughter some vital lessons about womanhood. Do not get me wrong, she was raised with core fundamental values including ethical and moral standards that are respectable to God and herself. I did my best to make her feel that she mattered, and she was my biggest priority, but I still missed the mark.

One lesson I have learned is that children do not come with a book of instructions, and this revelation gave me the serenity to confess that I missed the mark in a few areas. It was difficult to admit my own faults at first because blaming her father for each shortcoming was easier to do and accept. Honestly, I felt like I had a right to be the blamer and not the owner because I was the single Black mother that stuck to her responsibilities—the one that supports and protects others to a fault and forgives while repeatedly being mocked, persecuted, and undervalued. There was no doubt in my mind that I had a right to blame him for everything.

Despite my emotions telling me otherwise, I was wrong for not accepting responsibility. The part I played was performing as a "strong Black mother" and not genuinely being true to myself. I showed my daughter how to mask her feelings through laughter, jokes, and smiles. I taught her to stay active in sports, community events, and church functions while emotionally dying inside. I was the poster woman on how to allow people to take advantage while being broken, and I inevitably taught my daughter how to lie and undervalue herself.

Worst of all, I taught her how to lie to God when telling him "I trust you for everything."

It was *me,* and I accept my part. Looking back on my daughter's childhood there was no way I was equipped to teach her the significance of self-worth, self-identity, and self-respect because I did not believe in it for myself.

Through it all I was able to prevail. My daughter and I both benefited from professional family counseling. We didn't see eye to eye at the beginning. After many visits, we learned to understand and communicate effectively. It really pushed me to own my stuff. It took up until three years ago for me to admit my faults and flaws as a mother. It was not easy to let go of the stubbornness, but I learned the true meaning of self-worth. It became important for me to sincerely exhibit self-worth while teaching my daughter. Blaming others was not a pretty sight and it was not mature. It kept me blind and captive to the lack of identity, ownership, and respect for self. There were moments it seemed as if I lost the opportunity to be the example my daughter needed me to be, but contrary to what many people believe, there is still hope.

Now, I am mentally liberated. I am truly able to empower my daughter through her early stage of adulthood. I am equipped and capable to not only speak but live with assurance to thrive with God at the forefront. Today, I quickly identify any sense of feeling inadequate. I acknowledge it, and I take the positive steps to move forward. In having this mindset, I am prepared to help my daughter in her own journey. In this next chapter, I refuse to give in to what kept me stagnant.

Self-Discipline

Discipline is a consistent word for me in this season. In order for me to see change and positive results, there must be discipline. Not a little bit or 50-50, but it must be 100 percent pure discipline. The type of discipline I want is not going to come from riding on someone else's coattail. It also will not come in a form of a pep talk from family and friends. Self-discipline will have to be self-motivated.

It is awesome to be surrounded by supportive and positive loved ones, but they should not be the only driving force I lean on when fulfilling my goals. My supportive circle is beyond amazing. I always thank God for placing each of them in my life because they have kept me grounded. Each one of my loves inspired me to keep going, to make wiser decisions, and to see the beauty within myself. I lived on their motivational words for some time, but it was not enough. I had to find the strength within myself to be disciplined. I believe self-discipline builds character and confidence. It is good to be able to depend on others when necessary, but it is more uplifting when I can depend on myself. There were several instances that I relied on others and when things did not pan out the way I expected, I became frustrated. I shut down and lost confidence in myself. I made rash decisions, especially with finances. I depended on others so much for ideas on how to maneuver that I crippled my own discipline.

Ten years ago, there was a preacher from Virginia speaking in this church service in Pennsylvania. I went to the altar for prayer, and he said this scripture to me—James 1:8: "*A double minded man is unstable in all his ways.*" This preacher had never met me and did not know what my situation was at the time. He spoke it, and it confirmed that, due to my lack of discipline, I was unstable. In my unstable situation, I kept being stagnant day in and day out thinking that everything in my life will flourish one day. I just needed to be more creative, so in the beginning of each year, I had a vision board night with my daughter, where we would develop our new year goals. I loved the vision board night because it was one of our best bonding moments. It was filled with food, music, and great ideas. We would talk with excitement, and it was energizing to set family and individual goals. As excited as those nights were, I now realize we didn't plan how we would reach our goals. I learned the hard way that *no plan equaled no results.*

For example, one of the goals on the vision board was to be debt free and improve my credit score. Initially, I had signed up for various credit repair and credit counseling services, and even signed up for debt consolidation too. Each program started off good, but I would cancel the services when I felt like things were getting too hard for me to manage or when I listened to someone else's strategy on improving credit. I made excuses on why the plan didn't work. I didn't even give the services six months before saying, "No this isn't it. Let's try this other program." I lacked self-discipline. I prayed about being free from debt but did not create a plan. I lived in the revolving door, and it became old. I was getting annoyed with my own excuses. It was time for change.

One Saturday, I sat down at the kitchen table and reviewed my credit report from all three credit bureaus. I wrote down my current and delinquent bills and put a plan in place that same day. I took accountability for my actions and decided to no longer live a life of cycles. Since that Saturday, I have paid down several bills and even increased my savings. It had to start with me. I had to first discipline my mind and motivate myself to improve. My confidence has increased, and I know that with God and self-discipline, I can get positive results. There were times when the battle appeared lost, but I am finding victory in the war.

I even adapted a healthier lifestyle and am making more conscious choices when it comes to food. At the time of writing this, it has been 60 days since I cut pork, red meat, turkey, and chicken out of my diet. The next step is cutting bread and sweets. Those items are my weakness, but I believe in and encourage myself.

Purpose must come from within. Each day, I am making sure that I mentally push myself to remain disciplined. The more I remain disciplined, the more it helps me value myself authentically.

Self-Value

Self-value has been extremely crucial nowadays and reclaiming my life has given me a bold stride in cherishing my true essence. There were times when I was influenced by the appreciation from others. It gave me assurance. On the flip side, the lack of appreciation caused me to question my worth. I would question my first instinct time after time. Sometimes I still do.

Before the pandemic, it had gotten to the point where I saw my life as one big regret. Who wants to think in that manner? Let me answer the question, no one wants to purposely think and/or feel as if their own life is a regret. It is a depressing path of remorse, and life should be seen as paths filled with lessons instead of shame. I lived in shame for years and shame stole my self-worth. Living in shame made me feel low and unmotivated. Shame made me feel embarrassed. Shame wasted valuable time in many stages of my life. At this very moment, shame no longer resides in my space and it took a pandemic for me to find strength to stand in my truth.

I refuse to have the reflections of people, places, and things determine this chapter of my life. Most important of all they will not determine my future. How I perceive and treat myself determines my growth and prosperity. I want to prosper in every aspect of my life, so I have declared that I will no longer depreciate my value. I am affirming my self-value by appreciating me.

I will appreciate my genuine thoughts and compassionate heart.

I will appreciate my inner and outer beauty.

I will appreciate my many blessed talents.

I will appreciate my joy, happiness, and peace.

I will appreciate my unique style.

I will appreciate my voice that deserves to be heard.

I will appreciate transparency.

I will appreciate my vision and carry out my mission passionately.

I will appreciate my love for my daughter and the lessons learned as a single Black mother.

I will appreciate all of me.

Recently, someone encouraged me to change my language. They asked me what was going on and I responded, "Nothing." This person inspired me to change my response to "Everything." Here and now, let me change the *I will* to *I am*. *I am* walking with self-value, and I am thriving, unapologetically.

About *Dawn L. Pipkin*

Dawn is a native of Wilmington, Delaware. She is a mother of one child. She is an author of the non-fiction book titled, "MID HOUR." Dawn has a Bachelor of Arts degree from Lincoln University and an MBA from Strayer University. She is well known for having a compassionate heart, being humble, and helping others. Through personal life circumstances, Dawn found her true passion and gift to encourage others through the worst conditions. This passion has inspired her to start "Dawn of A New Day LLC." It is a business that provides inspirational literature, art, and go-to items for people who are experiencing anxiety, depression, and low self-esteem. Dawn is a warrior, and she refuses to give up. Her favorite scripture is Isaiah 54:17:

"No weapon that is formed against thee shall prosper; and every tongue that shall rise against thee in judgment thou shalt condemn. This is the heritage of the servants of the Lord, and their righteousness is of me, saith the Lord."

No matter what life may bring, Dawn L. Pipkin will rise above and soar.

Dear Diary:

"Walls are coming down and chains are being broken."

FORGIVENESS AND THE WOUNDED CHILD
Donyell M. Bruce Coleman

"If you weren't my mom, I would punch you in your fucking face right now!"

How would you respond if the person that you gave birth to naturally without any drugs said that to you?

My response? "Then forget I'm your mom and go right ahead!"

I was completely serious. We had just had a disagreement and the tension was high, but I couldn't understand why her response was so venomous. Little did I know, she was harboring resentment towards me for something that happened several years ago.

For so many years, my daughter loved me as her mother but hated me as a person, and I didn't know. She allowed a traumatic experience from her childhood to simmer in her spirit until she reached her boiling point and she exploded on me like a ticking time bomb. We were in Washington, D.C. and had just had a wonderful day visiting the National Museum of African American History and Culture as a family for her 27th birthday.

There were eighteen of us in separate cars in separate parking areas. I got back to my car and honestly forgot that I had my youngest granddaughter's car seat in my car. She was almost two at the time. Our next stop was dinner at a restaurant that was about four miles down the road. I left the parking garage and was on the highway heading to the restaurant, and my daughter called me on my phone asking where I was. I told her I was on the highway. She started screaming that I had the car seat and needed to return immediately to the garage. I told her I wasn't turning around and to just drive to the restaurant since it was so close. What she didn't know is that I was trying to figure out how to navigate back to the garage. Afterall, I was in unfamiliar territory.

Once I made my way back, she and her husband approached me yelling and cursing because I had the audacity to suggest that she drive her vehicle without a car seat for her child. They took the car seat out of my car and drove home leaving the rest of us to just continue on to the restaurant. I was honestly taken aback by the outburst and embarrassed as it happened in front of one of my good friends and her daughter. I couldn't figure out why the misunderstanding leading up to that explosion had caused her head to spin around like she was possessed by a demon. All of this over a car seat that I returned? She honestly thought I was serious about not turning around? I wouldn't know until a few months later.

Once we returned home, nothing was the same. My daughter wouldn't talk to me and I couldn't talk to her. She wouldn't even allow me to see my two granddaughters. This went on for about three months. It felt like I was in mourning. Some nights I couldn't sleep. I felt like I couldn't breathe. It was awful. My younger daughters who were 15 and 13 felt like the family needed an intervention, so we called a family meeting, and my daughter revealed that she never forgave me for what happened to her when she was 15 years old.

At that time, I was 34 and dating someone that was a few years younger than me. No big deal to me. My husband was younger than me and he had recently passed away. I started spending time with this person, more for friendship and companionship rather than a true love interest. We spent so much time together that he eventually started staying with us. A few months after he moved in, I became ill and was hospitalized. Once I was discharged and back home, I couldn't do a lot for myself. He, along with my daughter, was a big help with my younger children by cooking and cleaning. I appreciated his assistance. Little did I know the damage that was being done in the dark.

My beautiful, amazing, free-spirited baby girl came to me one day out of the blue and told me that she was being sexually violated by him. Not only was she being violated but so was her best friend, who at the time was also living with us because she was having issues at home and her mother had put her out. I was in disbelief. The person that I shared my bed with every night was doing the unimaginable to these children. I don't even think I had a response when they told me. I don't recall feeling anything. I'm sure my non reaction hurt and confused her even more. *Why would he do that? Why would he want a child? MY child at that?*

I didn't react right away. I didn't know what to do. They both left my home the very next day and went with my daughter's father. The police and the state were called in. An investigation went forth which lasted about a year, a year with no communication with my daughter. I walked around in a fog, still not sure how to feel, but I became more watchful of what was going on in my home. I had all my sight on my other daughters who remained in my home. They were two and four years old at this time, and I still had to be the happy mommy for them. They were innocent and knew nothing. They are now 15 and 17 and still don't know anything. The case didn't make the news, but some family knew about it and that was embarrassing enough. Only a couple of my friends knew. They were there if and when I needed to talk but I didn't talk about it. I kept all of my emotions bottled up inside. What could they do about it? Nothing. I suffered in silence and put on a brave face. It was no one's business but mine.

My beautiful firstborn who I loved with my entire soul and her friend who I was responsible for at the time were saying one thing and of course he was saying another thing. The results of the investigation said something else: *Accusations unfounded, no charges filed.* Well, what did that mean? Did they lie? I didn't understand. All I know is after a year of going through hell, I finally asked him to leave. I needed to put this nightmare as far in my rearview mirror as I possibly could. It was time to move forward and get on with our lives.

He left. She came back. Her friend was somewhere else. We never spoke about it again until the family meeting twelve years later. What she wanted from me was an apology for not doing anything on her behalf.

How do you ask for forgiveness when you don't know you've wounded someone? Does the need for forgiveness come immediately? For me, it didn't because I had to go back in time and check myself. I had to see where I was at fault. Did I see signs? No, I didn't. Did I suspect anything out of the ordinary? No, I didn't. The only tapes I kept replaying over and over in my head were the ones of my daughter's tears falling down her cheeks as she told me she had been violated by a man I allowed to stay in my home; a place that was supposed to be our safe haven. It was at that point that I realized that as a parent I had selfishly failed my child.

About a year and a half ago, my daughter and I sat down and had a conversation. Once we talked one on one with no distractions, she explained to me how badly that experience had affected her well into her adult years. She said she became overprotective of her oldest daughter who she gave birth to at age seventeen. She is very selective about who she is around and who she spends time with. Outside of family, overnight visits are not allowed. My granddaughter is now eleven and has only stayed overnight at one friend's house and that was after an extreme vetting process. She also shared with me that she has intimacy issues with her husband who she has been with for seventeen years and married to for six years. She has post-traumatic stress disorder due to the flashbacks of being assaulted. She feels guilty and regrets that she never had the courage to shout no without fear that the sexual assault would be turned around on her as she was constantly threatened. He told her that if she said anything, he would say she was lying and that she was the one coming onto him.

Even though she's married, she feels sexual intercourse is for reproduction only and not for pleasure. My daughter also feels like she failed her friend because her dad could only care for her for a couple of months. After that she went into foster care. Although her friend does not want her to feel this way, she feels like she's the reason her friend has made some poor life choices resulting in having three children with two fathers, living in homeless shelters, being in food lines, to now living in income-based housing with no car or job.

I went numb. I found myself in the same position as before where I didn't know what to say or how to respond which upset her again. She requested an apology from me *again*. She was under the impression that I took his side and not hers. This time the question in my head was different.

How do you ask for forgiveness when you can't admit that you've wounded someone?

After this conversation, there was still no resolution, apology, or forgiveness. I don't believe in apologies that aren't sincere. I felt awful seeing her leave, but I had some soul searching to do. What she didn't know was that I didn't take his side. I had not been in this situation involving my children before and I didn't know what to do. I wanted to fight him, scream, yell, hit something! But I didn't. I kept it in. You can look at someone else in the same or similar situation and profess to the world how you would handle it, but until you're in that situation you really don't know what you would do. I remained silent. I became like stone. I didn't even cry. I just went on with my daily life. Afterall, I had two other children to care for and look out for back then.

I had to be strategic in how I told him that he had to leave. I didn't know if he would become indignant and insist that he wasn't leaving since my daughter wasn't there. I didn't know if he would try to say that I couldn't put him out because he had been living there for so long. I just didn't know and didn't want a standoff. I just knew he had to go. I finally said this is it, you have to go, and he did. In hindsight, I would have handled the whole situation entirely different.

A huge "trauma bump" that I was unaware of was that after the incident in D.C., my daughter no longer felt comfortable allowing my youngest granddaughter to stay overnight with me as opposed to my oldest granddaughter. She said she didn't feel like I was capable of protecting her baby any longer. The D.C. incident triggered her PTSD and her childhood trauma. She associated my inability to protect her baby then to my inability to protect her now, causing paranoia. Talk about a WOW moment! I never knew any of this. My granddaughter is now four years old and has recently been allowed to stay overnight with me again. I appreciate my daughter's honesty, but that was truly tough to hear.

Although she is currently in therapy and highly recommends it, it hasn't helped her with this situation. What did help her was another heartfelt conversation that we had where I opened up to her about a situation that I dealt with decades ago. I too was in what I thought was a healthy, happy and safe relationship, but experienced sexual trauma. I never talked about it to anyone. I internalized it. After I shared this with her and how I dealt with it, she realized I wasn't equipped with the right tools to help her deal with what happened to her. This allowed her to forgive me once I finally gave her the sincere, heartfelt, and honest apology that she was longing for. This conversation was therapeutic for me, this was her moment of healing, and because of God's grace and mercy, our healing was just beginning.

This process was not easy by a long shot, but I am grateful and thankful for God's love for us. No matter how badly we mess up, His Fatherly love never leaves us. I believe in God and I have strong faith in Him. Over the years, I have learned that everything that we go through in life, whether good or bad, is part of our testimony. Many years ago, I stopped asking *"Why me Lord?"* and started saying *"I had to go through this to help someone else along the way."*

You can't change what you don't confront.

Since that initial confrontation, the family meeting, and the open dialogue with my daughter, I have become the protective mama bear over her cubs, and I do not play when it comes to any of them. I am selective about who I allow around them that is of the opposite sex. I have placed my dating life on hold, and I have no regrets. I can wait. I vet their friend's family and limit the time they spend with friends. I question *everything* and it gets on their nerves, but I don't care. They will thank me for it later in life.

I would not have shared this without my daughter's consent, so I have to take this time to thank her for being vulnerable enough to allow others into her world. I pray that what I have shared will help some mother that has to forgive or be forgiven.

As parents, we are not always right, but with the Lord's help, may we find the answers that we need in order to be the best parents we can be. Will we always get it right? Absolutely not. That's why we must turn our hearts to the Lord, ask Him for guidance, and listen to Him for instructions. He will never lead us astray and He will give us wisdom to make the right decisions.

"If any of you lacks wisdom, you should ask God, who gives generously to all without finding fault, and it will be given to you." James 1:5

"Bear with each other and forgive one another if any of you has a grievance against someone, forgive as the Lord forgave you." Colossians 3:13

About *Donyell M. Bruce Coleman*

Donyell Michelle Bruce Coleman is a native Delawarean. "Donnie," as she is affectionately called, is a proud mother, grandmother, and daughter. Raised in New Castle, Donnie matriculated through school and attended University of Delaware. Donnie wears many hats and has vast skill sets. She is a dental assistant, fitness enthusiast, procurement specialist, Uber driver to her kiddos, and devoted grandmother to her grandchildren. To know Donnie is to know she has and will move Heaven and Hell for her loves. Donnie shares her life with her children, Jordan, Seraiah, and Devon, and her doting grandchildren, Chloe, Riley, and Garrison. With much joy she has volunteered her time through her church, Get A Grip Teen Mentoring as well as Love in Action outreach ministry.

Dear Diary

"I feel a transition taking place in my mind and I find myself challenging my thoughts. This place feels good and refreshing!"

LOSS AND LESSONS
Erica M. Allen

Haruki Murakami is quoted saying "*Death is not the opposite of life, but a part of it.*" I have heard this statement in many ways throughout my 38 years on this earth. Simply put, we are all born, and we all die. While that statement may seem short and sweet, it is the in between that can dictate how one perceives death. I have experienced the death of loved ones throughout the years. As a child, my family would attend funerals often, as I come from a large family, so I was exposed to death at an early age, though at that point in time, I did not grasp the full concept of death I have learned over the years.

I began to grasp a better understanding of death in 1996 with the first significant loss of a loved one, my maternal grandmother. I was 14 and recently began my first year of high school. My grandmother had different medical struggles over the years but during this time things seemed more serious.

My uncle Tommy flew in from California but before he could arrive, my grandmother passed away. This showed me how things are not on our time but on God's time. I was preparing for school and the house phone rang so I answered it and my grandmother's doctor was calling for my mother. She wasn't home yet, as she worked night shift, so I called her and told her that the doctor had called. I had a feeling that the news was not good, so I stayed home to await my mom's arrival. Once she got home, she called and it was confirmed, her mother had passed away in the night. Oddly, my mom had visited my grandmother at the hospital on her way to work the night before and came out of the hospital to a flat tire. Later on, she explained that she

35

felt that the flat tire was a sign for her to stay with her mother as this would be the last time that she saw her alive. In hindsight, she wished she would have taken heed to the warning, but there was nothing she could do in the present other than regret her judgement. I felt her pain as I watched her grieve her mother. I tried my best to stay by her side as much as possible and do whatever she needed me to do.

We made funeral arrangements as a family and buried my grandmother within a week. My grandfather seemed lost without my grandmother as he depended on her for so much despite the fussing and bickering that was common in their household. It was now silent, and I imagine he didn't know how to handle the silence. From the death of my grandmother, I witnessed through my mom the toll that such a loss can have. They say there is no love like a mother's love, and this held true for my mom and grandmom. They spent a lot of time together shopping, cooking, going to church, and just being mother and daughter. Her loss left my mom empty, as she no longer had the first person she met when she arrived in this world and the person who had her back throughout her life.

In 2003, I lived with my grandfather. I had been back and forth between many different places as my mom's husband did not like me and put me out of his home multiple times starting when I was 13 years old. Living with my grandfather was interesting as he was very strict, and I had to follow his rules. Even though I was in my 20s, he was from the old school and what he said went. Well, for the most part because after a while, I had to show him that some of his rules were outdated.

He once locked me out of his house by locking the screen door, and I cut the screen door open to get through to the main lock. Being as though he was so stern, my family was highly entertained at my shenanigans, but I made it clear that I wasn't being disrespectful, I simply needed to get into the place that I called home. Another time he poured blessed oil used for anointing people for prayer on my cordless phone and it broke. When I asked him what he did to my phone he said he didn't like the conversations that I was having on the phone, so he had to anoint it. I was so angry, but again my family was amused at the tug of war that I was in with my grandfather. I thought I was grown, and he was determined to show me that I was not. Over the years that I lived with my grandfather there was a lot of pushing a pulling with the rules and regulations, but I am grateful for these memories as they shaped me into the person that I am today.

In April 2003, I was off from work for a doctor's appointment. When I arrived home, I had to settle some things with my insurance card, so I made my way into the house and as I was walking up the steps, I looked at my grandfather. He was sitting in a white plastic lawn chair in his living room with his bathrobe over his pajamas. His feet were crossed, and his arms were folded.

He looked at me as I laughed at him and said, "What you laughing at, girl?"

I said, "You. You have on a brown sock and a blue sock."

We both laughed and I went to my room to make a phone call. I wasn't in my room long, when I heard a loud thump. I sat still for a minute and yelled out to ask my grandfather what it was. He was like the neighborhood watch, so I knew he'd have an answer, especially since the thud seemed to shake the whole house to the point that I thought that a car hit us. But my grandfather didn't answer, so I got up and knocked on the bathroom door as I could see the light was on in there and I thought I recalled hearing him go in. My knock went unanswered, so I peered in through a crack that had been in the door forever, and I saw my grandfather laying on the bathroom floor gasping for air. I tried to get in the bathroom door, but I couldn't because he was wedged against the door. With him being a tall solid man, there was no way that I could make it through, so I called 911 and my mom. I was so frazzled that when the dispatcher asked me what the nearest intersection was, I could not remember, and I gave the wrong info. Calling my mom was awkward, as I had a conversation with her earlier that morning when she came over to check on my grandfather. We had been on the outs due to the division caused by her husband, and I didn't wish to continue trying to have a relationship with her at the time because I was troubled that she would allow a man to disrupt our relationship, not to mention, she was pretty much all I had since my father was in and out of my life. So, the disappointment had come to a head and I was fed up.

When I called, her husband answered the phone and I told him what had happened. I believe he put my mom on the phone, and she said she would be right over. I still remember the grogginess of her voice as she had worked the night shift and I probably woke her from a deep sleep.

It seemed like it took forever for her and her husband to arrive. My mom said that she felt as though she could have run to the house faster than the car would go. My mom's house was 0.2 miles away from my grandfather's.

When my mom and her husband arrived, he had to push through the door with all of his weight and get into the clawfoot tub, and then pull my grandfather up so that my mom could get in. Once she was in, they laid my grandfather down, and my mom administered CPR.

Once the paramedics arrived, they worked on my grandfather and carried him down the steps on a gurney-type thing because the stretcher was too big to fit up our narrow steps. When they loaded my grandfather into the ambulance and took off, we all went to the hospital. As I sped to the hospital, my brother called me saying that he had a flat tire, so I went back to pick him up. Once I got to the hospital, there were a lot of friends and family gathered. We sat and chatted. I waited for the doctors to call us back so that I could see that my grandfather was ok, but that never happened. Instead, they took us to a room and gave us the news that my grandfather passed away. He had a massive heart attack. I was shocked and dumbfounded. Not only had I not expected this to happen, I didn't know what was next and I was numb. I felt responsible for my grandfather's passing as I felt as though my rift with my mom stressed my grandfather so badly that it killed him.

My living situation had to suddenly change because I was scared to go back into my grandfather's house. This home was the home that my uncle, mom, brother, and myself grew up in, but I could not stay in the house by myself, and I definitely couldn't go into the bathroom. My family offered to let me keep the house, which was paid off, but once again, I just couldn't. Looking back, I regret that decision greatly because I could have had a three-bedroom home that held so much of my family history wrapped up in the walls. The fact that I couldn't, was a common theme after my grandfather passed away. *I simply couldn't.* I couldn't pull myself together to go to school and finish my Chemistry class because I thought I would fail anyway. Unbeknownst to me, the professor passed everyone in my class with a C. The fact that I couldn't caused me to delay becoming a nurse for over 14 years.

From the loss of my grandfather, I learned that tomorrow is not promised. Even the next minute is not promised. I praise God that the last moments of my grandfather's life were filled with laughter. My last vision of him alive is positive, so I always try to end with positivity at all costs. I try to avoid having bad blood with anyone as you never know when they will be gone. In addition, I learned not to give up. Had I not stopped attending school, I might have been where I wanted to be by now education-wise, but I have also learned that my time is not God's time. The way that things have played out in my life are the way that they should, so I have to refrain from questioning the way that things have transpired.

Many years after losing my grandparents, life had many ups and downs. In 2015, my son needed a heart transplant at the age of four months. This goes into the top five most traumatic experiences of my life. I suffered a loss prior to having my son in June 2015, so Eric is my rainbow baby. I specifically decided not to find out his gender so I could be surprised. I told myself that I was tricking the system, as I already had two baby girls and I really truly wanted a son.

Well, it worked, and God blessed me with my baby boy. He was born healthy as far as I knew but seemed to cry a lot and had several abnormal newborn screening tests. I was tired of taking him back and forth to get his heel pricked because I felt bad for him, but I wanted to ensure his safety. Nevertheless, the tests continued to be abnormal, but his pediatrician decided he looked good, so he would just continue to monitor him. On October 11, 2015, I decided to take him to the emergency room as he cried for what seemed like all weekend long. That morning, as he was swinging in his baby swing, his lips looked blue to me, so we jumped in the car and headed to the local hospital, which was five minutes away. They took him back quickly and tried some high flow oxygen, which didn't help and decided to do a chest x-ray. After it was complete, the doctor pulled me to the side and showed it to me. My son's heart was spread almost across his entire chest. I later learned that he had cardiomyopathy, a disease that causes the muscle of the heart to enlarge, which can weaken over time and be fatal. The doctor informed me that she was calling for the helicopter from AI Dupont to come get him as he was in critical condition. Seeing men come in with flight suits on, put my infant son on a bunch of machines, and wheel him off to their helicopter is something I will never forget. I had to put my son in the hands of strangers and trust that he would be okay.

The helicopter ride only took 15 minutes, but I was not allowed on due to safety precautions, so I had to travel by car. For a Sunday afternoon, there was so much traffic that it took forever to get from Dover to Wilmington. During the ride, a doctor called from the hospital and asked for consent to treat which I agreed. Then she called back and advised that I needed to get to the hospital as soon as possible because my son was very sick, and she asked me multiple times if I understood. I heard her and I was in route, but I couldn't get there any quicker. Once I arrived, I was greeted by my mom and my cousin. I broke down crying in both of their arms and waited to be allowed in the back to see my son.

Upon rounding the corner to the cardiac intensive care unit, I saw at least a dozen medical professionals surrounding a tiny patient and attempting to stabilize him. It was my son. He had been intubated and had wires coming from everywhere.

The doctor talked to me in a room across from the pod my son was in. She seemed so stressed and out of sorts that I had trouble following what she was saying, but I caught her three most important points. My son's heart was in really bad shape and he could get better and recover, he could need meds or another intervention and be ok, or he could die. It was essentially touch and go. Over the next few days, we met many different people, and the doctors ran many tests. It was determined that Eric had dilated cardiomyopathy and his only chance of survival was receiving a heart transplant. Some people hear heart transplant and think it is a fix, but we were educated that it is trading one illness for another and that it is not a permanent fix. Statistically, heart transplant recipients have a 50% chance of living until 20 years of age and this percentage decreases over the years. This was a hard pill to swallow, and I didn't want to believe it, but I had to rely on faith in this situation.

I kept going to church. My pastor would call me up for prayer and have me stand in proxy for my son. I prayed over and over through the nights and during the day. I told God that I would never drink another alcoholic beverage again in life if he let my son live. I only drank socially, but at this point I was literally bargaining for my baby's life. I would get on my knees anywhere and break out in prayer. My dad called me all the time and asked for updates. One day I told him flat out I was not going to bury my son and he asked me what I was going to do. I told him that my son was not going to die, he was going to live, and I meant that with every ounce of my whole entire being.

Our hospital stay began October 11, 2015, and Eric was placed on the heart transplant list on October 14, 2015. The transplant team was so excited that they were able to list him, but I was frustrated at their excitement. I didn't fully understand the depth of the situation and I didn't want to accept that my son needed a heart transplant. I even tried to transfer him to another hospital for a second opinion, but the insurance company denied the transfer. On Friday November 13, 2015, my mom and I were in Eric's pod talking. He was declining a bit, and I said "God, I wish you would just find a heart."

This was a troublesome thought for me as it meant that another little person had to die in order for my child to live and there were no guarantees that it would all work out at the end. Not long after I said that, the doctor and transplant coordinator came and watched Eric's monitors. I was concerned as I thought that they were going to deliver bad news. Instead, they nonchalantly said we have a heart that's being offered. I was like *wow, talk about express delivery.* I don't think a full hour had passed after making my request to God. Hearing this news was bittersweet, and my mom and I looked at one another in awe.

It was interesting how things played out over the next several hours. Members of the transplant team had to go and make sure the heart was a good option for my son, and once they confirmed that it was, they were on their way back with it. He was prepped for surgery and, all our family gathered to see him off. We prayed over him, we loved up on him, and we walked him to the operating room. This was a pivotal moment as they explained to us that there was a chance that he may not survive his surgery, so essentially it might have been the last time seeing my son alive. While my family was struggling, I had a calmness to me that could only be that of God. He had me be still. While we gathered in the hospital room, ate, and talked, I sat quietly and waited as we received updates from the transplant coordinator. They updated us on his progress, and I was able to see him. He was sedated and had even more wires and tubes coming out of him, but he was alive. Before I could take him home, I had to learn to take care of him on my own. He had to be lifted a certain way due to his chest being opened for surgery and he was on over a dozen medications throughout the day. But on November 27, 2015, he was discharged from the hospital and he has been doing well since. He is now five years old and in kindergarten. You wouldn't know his struggles by looking at him, but I say he is a miracle. He taught me that God is real, and faith will carry you through the hardest times of life. I remember hearing that you need faith the size of a mustard seed during a church sermon, and I have to say that faith and God's grace and mercy were and still are upon us.

In February 2016, I was still getting used to caring for my son along with my mother's help. One morning, I woke up to missed calls from my dad's girlfriend. Once I returned her calls, I learned that my dad had a stroke and was in the hospital. At this point I lived in Delaware, and my dad lived in Michigan, so I had to catch a flight to go see him. Upon my arrival, my dad was sleeping in his hospital bed. He woke up and saw me and started yelling. Due to his stroke, I couldn't understand anything that he was saying so he got frustrated and finally managed to say, "Go home!"

I asked him if he knew what was going on and told him that he had a stroke. He rolled his eyes and got frustrated. It took me a little bit to understand why he was upset that I was there but then I realized it was because he wanted me to get back home and take care of my son. Here this man was lying in a hospital bed after having a bleed in his brain and he was fussing with me about coming to see him because he wanted me to stay home and take care of my son. It made complete sense though. My son was named after my dad and he was so proud to have a grandson named after him. When my son was sick, he worried so much about him that he wanted to come from Michigan just to be with him. He was waiting for my son to be six months post-op to visit with us.

Once I made it home, I continued to check in on my dad. I would call him and try to talk but I didn't understand what he was saying outside of a couple of curse words that he could pronounce really well. I decided to obtain guardianship of him so I could move him to Delaware with me. He was in a nursing home and I wasn't fond of them, plus I wanted him to be close by so I and other family could keep a better watch over him. I got a court date for May 2016. On a few occasions I got calls from the nursing home saying that my dad fell. Because I visited him multiple times, I thought that this was strange as I never saw him try to get out of bed.

In May of 2016 while at the dentist, I got a call saying that my dad had fallen again. My blood pressure was so high that, had the dentist not heard the phone conversation, they would have refused to treat me. After that, I began calling the nursing home consistently to try to get answers about these falls, and I wasn't successful. Two days after the call while I was at the dentist, the social worker from the nursing home called and said my dad was declining so they wanted to put him in hospice care. I told her I'd come up and discuss it, so my mom, myself, and my three babies packed up and flew to Michigan. While on our way to the hospital, I got a call that my dad had coded and they were sending him to the hospital from the nursing home. They asked if I wanted him on life support until I arrived, and I agreed to it.

Upon arriving at the hospital, my dad was not on life support. He had an NG tube which had coffee grounds draining from his stomach. The doctor explained that he had a very bad infection and asked if I still wanted to put him in hospice. I agreed and spent the next couple of days in Michigan trying to get things together and visited with my dad. I sat in a conference room calling funeral homes while my dad was down the hall dying. I had to get things in order, but I failed to be in the moment and just be present with my dad. I had to get back to Delaware quickly as my son had a procedure to check his heart progress coming up.

On Saturday morning, I woke up thinking that I should go to the hospital and check on my dad before I left, but I was worried about missing my flight and didn't go. On the way to the airport the hospital called and said that my dad passed away. I felt guilty that he died alone but I comforted myself knowing that if he had to pick, he would have rather I be sitting with my son than sitting with him.

I had a lot of funeral preparation to handle. The life insurance that my dad purchased had lapsed and I had to handle things with my mom's help. It was such a blur, but I remember my aunt coming from California to help me through it. Between her, my mom, and God, I managed, but I will never be the same. I struggled with the relationship I had with my dad. He suffered from drug addiction which inhibited him from being the parent that I thought he needed to be, and I resented him for it. But after his death, I was able to find clarity in the fact that although my dad wasn't who I thought he needed to be parenting-wise, he was who I needed him to be. Even in his death, he has carried me through.

My dad's nickname was Rabbit, and a couple days after he passed, I was lost while driving. A big brown rabbit jumped out in front of my car once I found my way home, and I knew that it was a sign from my dad. Once I was accepted into nursing school, I was extremely nervous on my first day of clinical and almost quit. While on lunch, there were a bunch of rabbits just sitting by the walkway and I took that as my sign to keep pushing.

So, while he wasn't what I thought a dad should be, he was who I was supposed to have as a dad. His absence caused me to persevere through life and find my own way. I am forever grateful to him for his role as my dad. In addition, I am grateful for the lesson of not judging. My dad had a history that was beyond devastating and he survived the best way that he knew how. He struggled, but he never gave up, and that is why I keep going with all my might. I may waver, I may struggle, but I keep going.

In November of 2016, I learned that my mom was ill. We didn't know for sure, but it was highly suspected that she had a form of cancer. She had lost a lot of weight and began bleeding, but she had been post-menopausal for years, so this was irregular. In December of 2016, it was confirmed after a radical hysterectomy, that my mom had aggressive stage IV ovarian cancer that spread throughout her body. At this point in my life, I was in a practical nursing program finally pursuing that dream from 2003 of becoming a nurse. My mom was caring for my son while I was in school full time. I was only able to attend school in this manner as I had been laid off from my job due to a merger. So not only was my mom ill, but I was also facing the chance of having to once again quit school. I was determined to keep going though. God made a way and my mom got chemo but refused radiation. In no time, she was back caring for my son, was able to come to my nursing graduation in June of 2017, and she pinned me.

I made it; I was finally a nurse, my mom was in remission, and this was a blessing. While I knew that God was real, and my faith was a heavy part of my life based on my experiences with my son, I had even more faith after accomplishing a goal that I had for over a decade and seeing my mom survive something that could kill her.

Over the years, my mom went back and forth with chemo because her numbers would fluctuate, and in 2019, she unsuccessfully started a trial with oral chemo. This didn't work well for her, and I think at this point she gave up. Afterwards, she fell more ill. She slept a lot and couldn't eat much. In December 2019, she fell down the steps and had to be admitted to the hospital. This happened a time or two more and after a tough battle with pneumonia, she asked to be placed on hospice and declined further treatment for her cancer.

As time went on, she grew weaker and weaker. I had to watch her on a monitor while I was at work as I didn't have the option of not working because I had to support my household. It was the weirdest thing to be working as a nurse taking care of others when I really needed to be at home taking care of my dying mother.

In 2020, my mom declined significantly. The cancer had caused her bowels to be blocked so she would throw up when she tried to eat. She would also get impacted bowels and I would have to manually relieve her from her discomfort. In March 2021 with the onset of the pandemic, my mom was consistently vomiting. I had to change her, and I, myself had been battling pneumonia. I began staying home for my safety, my mom's safety, as well as my son's safety and the fact that my kids were all learning virtually.

Life became extremely different. I was tending to my kids and my mom, and I was overwhelmed. Hospice wasn't coming in as some of the caregivers were out with Covid-19, so care was all on me. I felt burned out. I expressed this to my mom when she began yelling my name and wanting me to sit with her. In hindsight I think that she was scared and didn't want to be alone, so I tried to be more present while also trying to shield myself from what was coming.

My mom was dying. I knew it as a nurse, but I didn't want to accept it as her daughter. We allowed the hospice nurse to come back in and she would let me know that the end was not far off. She educated me on the fact that what was transpiring was normal end-of-life behavior.

On April 2, 2020, a piece of me left this earth. I made sure that I was video calling family and close friends so that they could say their goodbyes. That day, I gave her a bed bath and lotioned her down. She liked her feet rubbed, so I paid special attention to them. I tucked her in and talked to my cousin and my mom's best friend, letting them know that the time was near. I noted the change in her breathing and advised my boyfriend that it wouldn't be long. Not long after that, I told my mom that it was ok to let go. I didn't mean it with my heart, but I meant it for her sake and moments later she took a breath, paused, took another breath, and she passed on. I held her hand until it was cool. I used my one hand to call hospice and the funeral home.

I see all of these things play out clear as day, but I am not ok with them. I want my mom. I miss my mom. I am in disbelief that she is gone. Death is permanent. There is no coming back from it and this particular death is one that I will never fully recover from. In my graduation message, I said my mom was my rock, but she was in fact more than that. She got me to where I am now. Her death has taught me so much and as a result, I have accomplished so much.

I used my grief as fuel to help me navigate and do some pretty amazing things such as start my own business and purchase my dream home. I married the most amazing man I have ever met and gained two bonus sons as a result. I try my best to be the best mom that I can be to my babies so that they can feel the feeling that I felt from my mom. I go to counseling twice a week to be present in my grief as I realize that I cope by avoiding it all together.

I am grateful for the lessons I've learned from all of my losses. While no one asks to be put in these predicaments, we have a choice of what to do with the remnants of grief. I have chosen to make positive life changes as a result of my losses. Whether it be increasing my faith, opening a business, walking in faith into a happy marriage, or building my dream home, I have allowed myself to excel despite it all. In all losses, there are lessons to be taught—we just have to be open to exploring their meanings.

About *Erica M. Allen*

Erica is a mother, wife, nurse, doula and more. She was born in Texas and raised in Kennett Square, Pennsylvania. Erica loves helping those in need, hence her career in nursing and birth work. Her happy place is the beach, she loves to listen to ocean waves, as they bring her peace amongst the storm. Over the years, she has learned many lessons, some of her most valuable being those resulting from the losses of those closest to her which have empowered her to continue to live life despite it all.

Dear Diary:

"Taking a minute to be reminded of God's faithfulness."

THE BORN CHILD
LaTesha M. Sam'i-Melton

I used to always ask myself, "*Why me?*" I didn't have a sense of worthiness growing up.

My mom and dad are from different sides of the tracks. My mom is a country girl, and my father was a city boy. They met "on the job" and fell in *lust*. They were young and in love or whatever.

My story began November 26, 1982. My loving parents, whose relationship lasted about 13 years or so, had a violent journey. I am not sure when the relationship turned completely sour; maybe when my mom found out another woman was pregnant at the same time as her.

She says, "Oh yeah, cheating was in full effect." Maybe it was also the lies, stealing, drug addiction, and now baby momma drama. Abuse became a huge factor in my mom and dad's relationship. I think the worse the addiction got for my dad, the worse the abuse got for my mom.

As a young girl, I remember my childhood being filled with fights and arguments. If it wasn't my mom and dad, it was other family members. It was rare to see love and affection in my family. I learned young that my mother's parents didn't like my father and my father side of the family didn't like my mom. It stemmed back to that baby momma drama and my dad having two women pregnant at the same time. I assume when this situation happens, families have to choose a side, so neither me nor my mom were lucky. I spent years trying to get "family" to love me not for who my mother or father was to them, but for who *I* was. I would sit and watch how my cousins would play so happily with my father's other daughter. They rarely played with me.

They rarely had anything to say to me. I sometimes forced myself on them just to be able to play like the rest of the kids. I used to cry and beg my mother to take me over to my father's side of the family, but the truth is they treated me just like how they felt I was to them: *a nobody.*

I was an innocent child. When children are innocent, they should not be subject to the pain caused by choices adults made. The lack of love from family was based on my parents, and that was a major bummer. I was born into a messy web with a lot of he said, she said. My father's sister told me to my face that she told other people that I was not my father's child. *Wow!* So, all the times I felt out of place at my relatives' houses as a child, with everyone being blatantly open showing love to who they wanted to love, I was not "tripping"–my feelings were very real. Meanwhile, it was easier for people to place blame on me, to prove points, or to say I was angry. Well, they were right. I was angry. *Very angry.* I could not understand for the life of me what I, LaTesha, personally did to these people. The trauma I endured from thinking I had done something horrible made my life as a child and young adult loveless. I did nothing but be born to an addict father whose addiction hindered him from being a father and to a mother whose father didn't show her love, so she sought love from men that were not worthy of her love.

My mom was sad and angry a *lot.* I remember times where my mom would not talk. She would sit in her room and stare at the TV, but I'm not really sure if she was actually watching it. If you would call out to her, she would not answer you as if the TV put her in a trance. When that happened, I knew not to bother my mom. I realized that my mom had her own childhood trauma and issues that she never sought help for. Time passed, and my mom ended up having two children by my father. After their relationship ended, my mom found that "love" thing yet again. A few years later I became a big sister again. This made four children for my mom. I have an older sister who lived with my grandmother. I heard it was because my mom was 17 when she had my oldest sister. Then when my mom got with my father, my grandmother did not like him. Maybe because my father was no good for my mom, maybe because of his addiction, or maybe because of his street lifestyle. Either way, my oldest sister did not leave my grandmother's house when my mom did. So, that put me up next for the oldest spot.

I spent my entire youth and teen years babysitting my two younger sisters. I hated it. Me and my mom did not have a good relationship when I was a teen because for one, I thought I knew everything. My gosh, I used to get so pissed because I had to have two kids with me most of the time.

I used to think to myself, "Yo, I am not the father of these damn kids. Where they daddy at?" My mom ended up marrying my baby sister's father. It's no secret I do not like him. He was worse than my biological father. He too had an addiction problem. Like mom, *really*? You get with a man with a drug addiction just like my father?

Life was becoming a cycle; my mom was mad a lot and always shut herself in her room. She would say hurtful things to me as a kid when she was mad. It was not until I became an adult that I heard the saying "hurt people, hurt people."

Out of all the hurtful things my mom said to me, the one I will never forget is my mom telling me her house is not big enough for me and her husband. Well, if you know an addict you know they get high and go to jail. That's the life of an addict. My mom's husband had just got out of jail doing like three or four years. For months I could never go to my high school games or work because I had to take care of two kids that I didn't birth. I finally got the courage to tell my mom how I felt about her husband. Not only did I tell her how I felt, I told her why I felt the way I did. This was her response to me:

"My house ain't big enough for both of y'all, so you can leave."

I remember thinking to myself, *"Me* leave? I'm the child here!"

I never wanted to kill myself, but I often wondered what life would be like if I didn't live. If God so loved the world, why did he give me this life with these parents and their family? I remember feeling like I would never be wanted by someone. My father didn't show me how a man should treat me. My mother didn't show me how to be a wife. Both of my parents married other people, but that's another story. So now I am a young adult in this world with no clue. I wanted to be loved unconditionally with no apologies.

I graduated high school and became a mother. I gave birth to my first child at the age of 19 and was in a relationship that was toxic. I played my part in this abusive relationship with my son's father. I knew it was not right, but it was normal for me because I was used to seeing and being around abuse. If someone would have asked me 25 years ago if I would be without my son's father, my answer would have been no. I was following down the same path as my mom, who appeared to follow down the same path as *her* mom. Even though I wanted to be with my son's father, I did not want the relationship we had. We were toxic for each other. We needed to let go. I thought letting go would make it better, but no, it didn't.

We went years battling with the co-parenting thing. So now everyone had an opinion about what they thought my life was going to be. I would hear the statement, "You gon' be just like your daddy," and I believed them. I felt like I had no direction for where I wanted my life to go. I remember crying myself to sleep one night, thinking "Damn, this is my life." Just me and my son. I knew I wanted to have a happy life at some point. I wanted to be a wife and a mother. I really didn't see the wife part happening for me because of the negativity I carried within. Family failed me. Friends failed me. Church failed me. Like, where do I turn? I worked hard to provide for my son. Co-parenting was one of the hardest things I had ever endured at first, but then I went from being homeless, to having bad credit, to working two jobs, to not being able to pay my utilities, to being told I made to much money to get help from social services, to just crying every night in the dark.

I found a peek of light just when I thought I could never love or be loved like how I imagined in my dreams when I was not having nightmares. I now call him my husband. I got married in 2004 and we both had nothing but our word that we would always have each other.

My husband and I both came into the relationship with a child. So yes, the baby momma drama came in full effect. When I say homegirl did everything in her power to break me and my husband as a unit, she did, but she also wanted to break him as a man. It was heartbreaking to watch the lows she reached. She could not break our union. We were in court so much that we were on a first-name basis with those working in the courts. I remember telling my husband that in time she will heal from the break-up and it will be okay. Well, I was wrong! She tried to have me arrested and fired from my job. She tried the silliest things to gain the attention of this man, my husband, who she claimed was always *her* man. I don't know why that statement was always funny to me, but nevertheless, our unit still stands in the face of those who doubted us.

My husband taught me the true meaning of forgiveness and love. We are about six years apart in age, and I am always eager to learn from him. My husband is not innocent; he wreaked plenty of havoc in his day, but he uses his experiences to teach our children. We've come a long way. We were homeless together and we both worked two jobs trying to pay bills. The struggle has always been real. I am blessed that God so loved the world that He gave me such a man. A man who could deal with the highs and lows of becoming a father and never giving up on his child. A man that took the role of head of household so seriously, that he took on everything. A man that, when his wife kept having health issues with her hair and skin, he drilled into her how beautiful she was and will always be in her natural image. A man that stayed up during the nights for feedings with his children when he was the one who had to work the next day. A man that helped his wife understand and get all the help she needed when she was diagnosed with severe anxiety and depression in 2010. A man who said, "*She is not perfect, but I love her.*"

Seventeen years later, I am still happily married, living life on my terms, free and clear, and no longer holding onto the anger that once held me hostage in my own mind and heart. After years of counseling, I am finally able to let go and live. This was so hard for me to do because I wanted answers. I wanted those people to own up and speak on how messed up they treated me when I did nothing but be born. Then I realized they didn't share the same hurt and pain as me. They may feel like they did nothing wrong, and if this is the case, then I will be the only one feeling angry for the rest of my life. Oh no.

I have to admit, after all the rejections and lies, I have learned to deal with people how they deal with me. I cannot hold people accountable for something they don't see is wrong. I forgive on apologies I will never receive. I had to forgive so I could share my story without crying and allowing anger to take over me.

After retraining my brain to think happy thoughts and saying something nice about myself every day, I now know that I am not what people thought of me. *I am not a failure.* I can proudly say my husband and I raised all our children. We are a team! I am at every game, parent-teacher conference, play, drill, show, etc. for all our children. I wanted to turn my negativity into positivity for someone else. I am the founder of a non-profit organization with the mission to build, restore, and solidify the bond between mothers and daughters through effective community linkage, crisis stabilization, and resource management, and it all stemmed from my relationship with my mother.

It turns out November 26, 1982 was the beginning of my life journey that was meant to bring me to where I am today—wife, mother, entrepreneur. Wow! *Me!* I would have never thought. People tried so many things to break me, and it worked. I was broken for so long. I didn't even know how I was going to put the pieces of me back together. I thought I could just move on and forget because most of this happened when I was a child. I tried to forget any of it ever happened, but I couldn't. I am glad I was able to get the help I needed to process this trauma. God gave me these experiences to be able to share and help another mother and daughter heal.

About *LaTesha M. Sam'i-Melton*

LaTesha, born and raised in Richmond, Virginia, is a wife and mother of four. After graduating from Richmond Public Schools, LaTesha worked in the mortgage field. LaTesha enjoys helping people, so she switched her focus to working in the communities. LaTesha is the Founder of 3 Nique Girls, Inc., a non-profit that focuses on positive interactions between mother and daughter. LaTesha is a Certified Community Health Worker and is an active member of the Virginia Community Health Worker Association and National Association of Community Health Workers. LaTesha also serves on the Henrico/Hanover Reentry committee. In addition, LaTesha serves as Vice Chair at Central Virginia Healthcare Association. When LaTesha is not serving her community, she enjoys family time and traveling.

Dear Diary:

"Took time away, still so much growing to do on this journey!"

BREAKING THE CYCLE
Naysia Fils-Aime

I was raised by my father's family. His aunt was the closest mother figure that I ever had and because of this, I call her "Mom" and consider my older cousins my siblings. My dad and I were inseparable from the moment I was born. My birth mother left when I was about two years old, and when I was five years old, I went to live with my family. During those years, I talked to my dad on the phone, and he would visit every now and then. It hurt me over the years because it felt like he didn't want to see me, and it felt like he didn't care about me. *How could he not care about his first-born child?* I was constantly told that my father was a liar and that he was running around doing all kinds of crazy things and hanging out with the wrong people. So, I guess, in a sense, I was being protected from all of that.

During my middle school years, I was a pretty happy, outgoing teenager. I played basketball and hung out with my friends, but that was just on the surface. Underneath it all, I was struggling mentally and emotionally. My home life was falling apart. My older siblings were all away in college and I was the only one left at home with our parents. They were going through a rough time in their marriage, and I witnessed the constant arguments and all the petty ways they would get back at each other.

I felt completely alone. I have always been a private person and never really felt the need to share things with my friends—even with my closest friends at the time. I never felt comfortable talking with guidance counselors either, so I just kept everything to myself.

After beginning 7th grade, things just got worse. In school, I was missing homework assignments, getting poor progress reports mailed home, and failing tests and quizzes. I remember getting a "D" as my final grade in my science class. I never brought home a "D" in my life, and that's when I started to hide my grades. This was the only time anyone ever paid attention to me—whenever I wasn't doing well in school or lying about the littlest things. I was constantly being compared to everyone in my life.

"Why can't you be more like your siblings?"

"You're just like your father, grandfather, and uncle—you're all liars. Do you want to end up like them?"

At home, the arguments were getting worse as well. Everyone was hiding things from each other and doing secretive things and in turn, I thought that was normal. For most of 7th grade, I stayed over my cousin's house, but it got to a point where I just didn't want to go over to his house anymore, and no one would listen. I just wanted to stay at my own house and do my own thing.

One day in my English class, my teacher wanted all of us to write a poem. I believe this was going to be a collection of poems from my class that was going to be "published" in the school's library. We had to use metaphors, similes, etc., and I wrote about everything I was going through during that time. I wrote about everything I felt during that time. I wrote about not wanting to live anymore without actually writing the words. That was the very first time in my life where I was my most vulnerable.

Looking back, that poem was a cry for help. I didn't think that at the time. All I saw was this beautifully written poem that I just knew my teacher was going to love. I never received any feedback about my poem. My teacher never talked to me privately about it. One of my classmates—a friend of mine—told me that *I* had to write another poem because ours were too similar, and that crushed me. To this day, I still don't know what happened with my original poem. All I wanted back then was to feel seen, heard, and loved. It was also during this time that I was being taken advantage of by a trusted adult. Throughout my life, I brought up the subject on numerous occasions, but just like so many other situations in my life, nothing has ever been done about it and in turn, I have never been able to truly heal from that experience. I carried all of this with me all through my teenage years, but thankfully, my home life improved while I was in high school.

During my freshman year of college, I lived at my school. I will honestly say that I took all of that for granted and soaked up every ounce of that freedom. I wasn't attending any of my classes. I mainly stayed in my dorm room or the library, attended club meetings, and hung out with my friends whenever they had free time. I ultimately flunked out, moved back home, and took classes to become a nursing assistant. Dropping out of college was yet another failure of mine added to a long list of failures and my mom constantly reminded me of that. I ended up landing three jobs, working my tail off to save money for a car and other things. During all of this, I reconnected with a high school friend, who has been my boyfriend for the past seven years and is the father of our two children.

Everything was perfect around this time. I left one of my jobs to pursue one of the other jobs full time and saved money to put a down payment on my very first car all while dating my amazing boyfriend who showed me what true love should look like in such a short amount of time. To this day, I still don't know what caused things to change in my life so abruptly, but sure enough, they did. One night, my mom and I had a huge falling out, and I decided that I needed to leave. It got to a point where I was done being treated like a young child. This was another moment in my life where I needed to be listened to; I needed to be heard. I was tired of being mistreated. It was not an easy decision, but I knew that I needed to finally be on my own.

Now, I knew where I needed to go from there. I knew I needed to go to my dad. At the time, he didn't know what was going on and on top of that, he and his aunt (my mom who raised me) were not on the best of terms. A big part of me felt that if I went to my dad, it would just make this whole situation worse than it already was. My boyfriend knew everything that was going on, talked to his mother, and she allowed me to live with her. I am forever grateful for her because she didn't have to help me out like that. My boyfriend and I lived with his mother and siblings for about two and a half years. I remember being told that I solely left my house to be with my boyfriend. While this is true—I knew if I had stayed, we would not be together now—I didn't leave *just* to be with him. I left because I needed to be my own person and truly be happy for once. I definitely didn't want to leave the way that I did, and it's something I wish I had done differently. From the way I handled the argument with my mom, to moving out and living with my boyfriend and his family, all of this deeply affected my relationship with my boyfriend.

We've had our own place now for almost three years, and this year will make six years since I left my childhood home. These past six years have not been easy in the slightest. I took my freedom and independence for granted and struggled to keep my responsibilities afloat and had trouble budgeting and paying my bills. I admit that these things are still somewhat of a struggle for me, but back then, I was in a different frame of mind. My mom and I never truly moved on from our falling out. The tension is still there, but subtle. It felt as though we swept all of that under the rug and never sat down and truly discussed what went wrong. That alone lingered in the air for a long time and still does. I wouldn't mind having this discussion with my mom, but I feel like even now, my voice would not be heard, and my feelings would be invalidated. I come from a West Indian/Caribbean family. In our culture, it's uncommon to sit down with our parents and talk about our feelings and our mental wellbeing. These conversations get dismissed, swept under the rug, and pushed aside.

When I found out that I was pregnant with my daughter four and a half years ago, I was scared for so many reasons. I was worried about how everyone else around me would take it and worried that everyone would tell me to have an abortion. Out of every conversation I had, some of the most meaningful conversations were with my older sister, my stepmom, and my boyfriend's mom. They all told me that the choice was mine and I have the right to do what I feel is right with my body, and I have held on to those words ever since. I was scared to tell my mom because I wasn't sure how she would take it. Her and my boyfriend had an exchange of words when I moved out. I was afraid of disappointing her all over again because I always felt like I spent my whole life disappointing her. She surprisingly took the news very well and it really made me feel great about my pregnancy. Other people in my family voiced their "concerns" but at the end of the day, I didn't let that affect me, as this was my life, not theirs.

I always went to visit my mom whenever I was off work. I would even bring my daughter along too. Our visits and our time together were great for the most part. These visits gave my mom a glimpse of what I was like as a mother with a child of my own and she told me every now and then that I was doing a great job with my daughter. During other visits, my mom would spend most of the time talking about all my past mistakes and how I hadn't changed much; and about how I spend too much time with my dad and my stepmom, despite her also telling me that I should continue to have a relationship with them. These visits brought me right back to my childhood–her constantly comparing me to other people and talking down on my dad and his family all over again. It was all so overwhelming for me and the worst part was that my daughter was present, listening to her mother being talked to in such a negative way.

I truly believe that all of this caused my daughter to cry around my mom. She would always cry and not let my mom hold her for a long time. During one of our visits, my mom asked my daughter for a hug, and my daughter said, "No." She was about one and a half years old at the time. Because my daughter said no, my mom told us to leave. She was upset that my daughter didn't want to hug her, even though my daughter hugged her earlier during the visit. My mom told me she was upset that my daughter enjoyed being around my dad and stepmom more than her and because of that, we had to leave. I didn't say anything, but I should have. I should've said that my daughter lives with her dad and sees him all the time and refuses to hug him sometimes. *Her own father.* I should've told my mom that my dad and stepmom don't treat me the way she does in front of my child, but I didn't say anything. I took it like I always did growing up, and I left. The worst part is that this should've been the moment I paid attention to my daughter's feelings and established some boundaries with my family. But I didn't, and I deeply regret that.

I had a miscarriage during the beginning of 2019. I was pregnant for a really short time. Everything happened so quickly that I never truly processed the feelings. I remember talking to my mom about it and she was upset because she wasn't the first person I told about my miscarriage. I remember her telling me to basically get over it and that I wasn't the only person that this has happened to. I was so confused about what I should be feeling at the time and to be told to get over it, I was crushed. My mom and I grew distant with each other; we barely called or texted each other, and I stopped visiting.

Later in the year, I found out I was pregnant again. I was scared this time because my boyfriend and I were going through a rough time, were trying to patch things up, and we felt like we weren't ready for another child. I honestly contemplated having an abortion and that was part of the reason I went to my dad's house one weekend. I followed my intuition and knew that I needed to keep this baby, which we eventually found out was a boy. This pregnancy was rough compared to my pregnancy with my daughter. My son was bigger, which made me bigger, and I had a couple of minor health concerns and was admitted in the hospital around 25 weeks pregnant. My mom and I still weren't talking, and I ultimately told her about my pregnancy when I was seven months pregnant.

My siblings invited me to a family holiday dinner since I hadn't seen or talked to anyone in quite some time. A part of me didn't want to go but decided to. My mom and I barely talked. The only exchange we had was her telling me she was upset that I didn't get up to say hi to her when she walked right past me without acknowledging me. After this dinner, I went on to give birth to my son right at the beginning of the first Coronavirus lockdown. This was a bittersweet time since I couldn't have the rest of my support system with me in the hospital.

About a month or two after giving birth, my mom called. Looking back at this phone call, this was when I began to subtly establish some boundaries. At one point during the call, my mom asked about my daughter and I told her that she was napping. My mom told me to call back when my daughter woke up, but I didn't. First, my daughter was not home, she was with my boyfriend's mom. Second, my mom didn't call or text to wish my daughter a happy birthday two months prior and is now asking about her? That truly rubbed me the wrong way. That was the last conversation I had with my mom.

I stopped talking to most of my family members and even blocked some on social media. This was my way of setting boundaries with my family. A part of me feels I could've gone about it a different way. However, I feel like if I did go about this another way, I still wouldn't have been heard or listened to and my boundaries wouldn't have been respected. It came to a point where I needed to focus on me and my little family more and protect them from toxicity. My pregnancy and the birth of my son made me realize that. It truly felt like a huge weight lifted off my shoulders and a dark storm cloud moved away from my relationship as well. I no longer had to worry about outside forces attempting to control me and my relationship. I no longer had anyone talking down on me and my life decisions. For the first time in my life, I truly felt, and still feel free and in complete control of my life. For once, I feel like I'm living my life the way I'm supposed to. For once, I'm finally focusing on me and bettering myself mentally, spiritually, and emotionally. In turn, this has created a positive shift in my relationship with my boyfriend, has helped me approach various aspects of my life differently and work on becoming the best mother possible to my babies.

For a time, I didn't want to become a mother. Dealing with abandonment and constant rejection from my own birth mother, I was always unsure if I would ever be able to love a child and thought about what if I abandoned my child? I always knew in the back of my mind that I would be different but decided it was just best not to have children at all. After getting to know my boyfriend better and being convinced that we were soulmates, I knew at some point we would have children together. Both of our children are the greatest things to happen to me.

As parents, one of our roles is to teach our kids. However, I feel as though my children have been the ones teaching me. My daughter has marched to the beat of her own drum ever since she was born. She was born three weeks early and her birthdate was actually the date of our baby shower. She's very meticulous about everything she does and makes sure everything is as perfect as possible. She is very adamant about her decisions and rarely ever changes her mind about things. She has taught me to stand up for myself more and face tasks, decisions, and various situations head on and be firm about whatever it is I want.

My son is very easy going and goes with the flow. He's down to try new things and is such a happy baby. Ever since he was a newborn, he has always been determined to take on tasks "bigger" than him. From rolling over during tummy time, to crawling, and now, walking. Once he sets his mind on something, he never gives up—no matter what. He gets right back up and tries again. He has taught me to be open to trying new things and expand my horizons. He has taught me to stop giving up on myself and my dreams and to always have a positive outlook on things. I am beyond grateful and blessed every single day that they both chose me to be their mother and that we have each other to grow and learn with.

As I sit here and reflect on my life thus far, I see what I want to be different for my children. I want them to feel seen, safe, and loved. I want them to feel comfortable talking to me about anything without fear, shame, or judgement. I didn't have that growing up.

I found a post recently that said something along the lines of, "If your child is acting out/not acting like themselves, that's their way of letting you (the parent) know that something is wrong." That's why, when that happens, it's important to sit down with them and discuss what's wrong, as opposed to lashing out at them and punishing them for their "bad behavior."

There's a reason why they were acting that way. By sitting down with them and having a discussion, you will make them feel valued, loved, seen, and heard. I grew up thinking and believing the "your children aren't your friends" concept. While it is true, I believe you should be friends with your children to an extent, with boundaries, of course. Having that connection with your children builds a certain level of trust that you may or may not get without that connection. I want my children to know that it's okay to be different and that it's okay to follow their own path. I want them to know that the world is theirs and they have options and should never limit themselves. I want them to feel comfortable in their own skin, to love themselves inside and out. I want them to embrace their flaws and understand that it's okay to feel things.

I've seen many people say that you should heal yourself before you have children. The healing journey is a never-ending journey and there's no correct way to go about healing. For me, my children helped me begin my healing journey. After becoming a mother, I finally started to see things for how they truly are. When people talk about generational curses, establishing generational wealth is always the forefront of the conversation. While generational wealth is important, so is breaking generational curses surrounding childhood trauma and other unhealed experiences. I've learned that in order to obtain the wealth you desire, you need to focus inward. Surround yourself with positivity, positive people, and positive thoughts. When you emanate positivity, it comes right back to you. When you surround yourself with negativity–toxic relationships and environments or telling yourself negative things–all you will attract is negativity.

I'm in a much better place now than where I was three years ago or even 10 years ago. I've learned that it's time to let go of the past and learn from all the mistakes made. Not just the mistakes of others, but mine as well. I've spent a long time resenting a lot of things that were said and done to me but I'm in a place where I can embrace all of the hurt, pain, and trauma, and turn them into something positive.

I can't change the past and I understand now that everyone tried and did the best they could for me at the time. Now is the time for me to pick up the pieces and do what's best for me and in turn, teach my children the same.

About *Naysia Fils-Aime*

Naysia Fils-Aime is a 27-year-old stay-at-home mother of two beautiful children, ages 4 and 1. She recently started her own business selling nail polish. After discussing what was written in Naysia's chapter, her relationship with her father is in a great place. They are extremely close and are continuing to heal from the past together. Naysia continues to live with her loving and supporting boyfriend. They look forward to beginning a new journey with their children in a new city and state within the upcoming year. She hopes to own more than one business in the near future. As Naysia continues on her journey of healing, she remains distant from the rest of her family.

Dear Diary:

"Above all else, his salvation is most important."

POSITIONED FOR THE PROMISE
Selara Gatewood

She took care of everyone's children, so why did hers have to die?

Emmanuel

In January 2005, I was planning a funeral for my mother-in-law, Pearl Yvonne. I had to stop working on the obituary because of my doctor's appointment. They were ready to admit me then. Since my blood pressure was too high, Christiana Hospital would not let me leave for at least an hour. The ground was frozen, and the streets of Wilmington were filled with ice. It was a bitter cold, like Poconos Mountains kind of cold. We were saddened because Curtis just reunited with his mom and now, she was gone. Last September or October, she told me she dreamt of rabbits. She looked up at me and said, "You're pregnant."

Thursday, March 3, 2005, Christiana Hospital declared Emmanuel stillborn. My small boy, my sweet small baby had a slow heartbeat, and they said they saw this all the time. They didn't even try to give him oxygen to strengthen his lungs. Earlier that afternoon, I experienced the worst pain in my life. Only 24 weeks. *Emmanuel, what's going on in here, son?* I thought. I arrived at the hospital on the corner of Washington and 12th Street. What could be the reason why they didn't treat a huge pregnant woman in excruciating pain who eventually threw up in the waiting area of the emergency room? Finally, when they took me to the back, they checked me, then rushed me to Christiana Hospital in Newark, Delaware. It is there I find out what I was made of. It's the chapter that changed me. I didn't understand this. *How can*

I be there for everyone's child and mine not make it? Who is this for, God? I made it a point to get married first, no premarital sex *just* so that my children and children's children could have strong lineage-breaking chains. Christiana Hospital explained that there was nothing they could do. Those words became dark and faint. *What do you mean? Did you try?* This was the first time I had ever heard of an incompetent cervix. I opened too early.

They said, "If this happened at 26 weeks, we would be able to do something like bed rest." *You are telling me only two more weeks constitutes viability?* Now, they just wait until it's time to push. My baby boy was not an emergency to anyone.

This is hard y'all. I had to deliver my baby boy. I told them to leave him in his incubator and in the room with me. I was up all night praying and talking to God. My relationship with the Lord is so intimate; I talk with my Father as if we are going out to eat and I just share, and yet on this Thursday night, I felt like I was saying God please talk back to me.

"I'm asking for a miracle. Prove the doubters wrong. Let them change the narrative that they see this all the time. Make me the exception. Lord, who in the Bible went through this? Was it the Shunammite woman? I need to know how to pray right now. Root out all my emotions so I can hear clearly and see a miracle happen now. Strengthen his heartbeat so I can take him home tomorrow morning."

Still, I don't hear God speaking back to me, letting me know everything is okay. I need to hear, "Daughter your faith has...", "if I did it for Jairus' daughter, I will do it for Emmanuel who still has a heartbeat."

"Lord you told Lazarus to get up. You worked through Elisha on behalf of the Shunammite woman. My baby's heart is slowly pumping. Come on, strengthen his lungs, Father." Every time I would go deep in prayer, Emmanuel's monitor went off. I'd stop praying, look over at his chest and go back in prayer. This happened about three or four more times. I would have to stop praying because his monitor's alarm would go off. I wanted to hear him cry and make some sort of sound.

Please Lord! I was not tired at all. Pastor Phil walked in my hospital room.

He heard me and said, "Whew! Daughter, your faith is strong in here." Curt was with me the whole time in the room sleeping or grieving quietly at the bow window. Pastor Phil and I talked, and he prayed for me. We talked some more, then he had to leave because it was late at night and visiting hours were over a long time ago.

I think I finally went to sleep from six to eight in the morning. The nurses came in to check on me and to prepare the discharge papers for 11 a.m. My heart was hurting to leave my baby boy at that hospital.

This is the root of my pain, even today. I walked over to say goodbye to Emmanuel, and it alarmed me to see his mouth wide open. At what time did this happen? Was it while I was praying? Was it when the monitors were going off? The tears I now shed that morning are for, "*I should have laid my hands on him and held him on my skin. I should have got up to check on Emmanuel when the monitors went off. I should have talked to him more, kissed him.*"

This whole ordeal should have brought Curt and I closer, for we both had just lost our firstborn. Instead, we grieved separately.

Three weeks later, Saturday, March 26, 2005, I was right back at the place of pain, Christiana Hospital, for my sister, who delivered a healthy baby boy. It took everything in me to bottle up the tears and be happy for her bundle of joy. On Easter Sunday, I brought Shanelle and Yusef, my niece and nephew, to see their baby brother, Isaac, and their mommy. I decided to breathe and live again. I chose life and to continue loving on other people's kids. Just as Emmanuel made it back in the arms of Jesus, I would continue to teach all the children around me to love Jesus.

Eden

Wednesday, September 28, 2005 Gianna was born to my sister, Makema, just weeks before Eden was supposed to be born.

October 2005. This cannot be happening again, and in the same year! Lord why!? Something happened that caused me to be hospitalized. One day I woke up in Christiana Hospital and my belly was soft. Well, that is very unusual. *Baby girl, what's going on in there?* They had monitor belts on my belly. Why were they not alerted to come in here to check the heart rate, pulse, or anything? I had never heard of a pregnant belly deflate. Physically, I felt fine. Just waiting for these two weeks to pass so I could be "viable." As I pressed that call button, the nurse told me to open my legs. A small piece of my umbilical cord came out. That was abnormal. I was dilated and didn't know it. She looked at me sorrowfully.

I said, "Well just slowly push it back in me."

She said she couldn't do that. "We have to induce you to deliver her. She is stillborn."

I better not hear those words again! Stillborn!? Are you telling me she is breathing, and you won't help her, or you can't help her?

I was wheeled into another room for preparation. While they said they couldn't push the cord back in, I remember something like a suppository having to be inserted in me to help the process. Because Eden was only one pound, I had to do most of the work. The contractions were very strong. This was the absolute worst affliction I had ever felt. At the time, Ms. Lane, Minister Moody, my spiritual brother, Walter Harmon, and I think his wife were there. They were over my bed talking to me and praying for me. Ms. Lane gave me a gift bag. I was in too much agony to look at it. *Baby!* when those pains hit, it was like an exorcism. There was great lamentation, throwing up, moaning, twisting, and turning. No matter what, my Wilmington Christian Center family was there.

Now this was it. Everyone had to leave so I can mourn this process alone. It was almost time to push. This was the longest undertaking to go through. Eden could not push her legs to slide down; she was so small. I had to get over it and align my body to get her out safely and breathe correctly so I may live. Finally, my perfect little angel was out. My little mocha was so beautiful with smooth silky hair, and brown toned skin. She was tiny. Amazingly I carried so high as if to be incubating a six-month-old, six-pound baby. She was in the sixth month of pregnancy but was only one pound. With all the appointments I had, could they not see that then? I was hurting and grieving because I remember the emptiness of leaving Emmanuel in the hospital, now Eden too. Later that night, I opened my gift from Ms. Lane. I was shaking because the sculpture was an angel with wings. It looked exactly like Eden–same complexion, same hair mold with a beautiful yellow dress smiling at me. *Oh My God!* I got the sculpture before Eden was delivered. How did Ms. Lane know to give me a gift reflective of my now deceased daughter?

I know that my children are powerful.
The devil is so afraid of them coming into this world.

I felt for the first time a deep depression until I received a phone call from Pastor Mamie Gamble. She wouldn't take, "I don't want to talk to anyone" lightly.

She said, "I've been watching how you take care of other people's children. Let me tell you–can't nobody take better care of your children like God can." Once I got that visual, that glimpse of my children happy and with God, I got up out of the pool of sweat and tears, I went upstairs, took a long shower, and apologized to my then husband for pushing him away. I felt terrible. I didn't consider his feelings. He was going through as much as me. His first child, his first son, and now his little girl. Once again, we grieved differently. I had turned down every call. I even pushed aside every gift basket, edible arrangements, and flowers that arrived at my door. *What was the point? Pray for what? My babies are not here. Why does everyone keep saying, "I'm sorry"? Did you have something to do with my children dying?* I was frustrated with hearing "I'm sorry." I shut everything out for a moment until Pastor Mamie Gamble bullied her way into caring for us. Her words helped me to see that the first fruit of my womb made their way right back to God, and that I was blessed.

Curt blamed me for their death, saying I should not have been busy at church and at work. He eventually turned back to substance abuse, something he had been clean from for quite some time.

Hannah Hephzibah
"God's Grace and Favor on Us"

It is not long before I hear the diagnosis again: "You're Pregnant!"

I didn't want to tell anyone I was with child. We regularly attended Wilmington Christian Center Church after New Destiny Fellowship service on Sundays. On Thursday nights, we were deep in Bible study with the Davenports and after the second service, I pulled Pastor Phil over to tell him the news.

He said, "We are going to do things differently this time. You are going to take your medicine." I knew exactly what that meant. I am going to speak the Word of God over my situation and my body. He gave me a book on confessions by Charles Capps about healing. This small leaflet book had powerful scriptures on different ailments in the body with scriptures related to it. It taught me how to have enough faith that God will do it for you; it's not enough to just know some scriptures but that it will come to life for you. In the end, there was a total body confession. I took my prescription morning, noon, and night. I recited this confession three times a day until I had it memorized in my heart. My body had to obey the power my tongue confessed over and over. Faith comes by hearing the Word of God. I took my prescriptions until Hannah's due date. *Do you hear me?* I went from having an incompetent cervix to needing to schedule her out. I knew she would come when she was good and ready–her due date!

Well let me back up a bit. I do not remember how many months I was when my doctor suggested I get a cerclage. A cerclage is a procedure, known as a cervical stitch that prevents premature delivery. Considering the history of carrying low and the outcome, we agreed to the procedure. The thing that made me nervous was the epidural. I didn't want it, but everything we do is for the baby's well-being. There was a peace that one could not explain. She talked to me during the preparation. It was all done. I didn't feel the pinch or anything go in my spine. She then flipped my bed in an upside-diagonal position to make sure my baby goes in the other direction away from stitches. My personal business was in the air for a few students to witness how to perform a cerclage. You know she has to be delicate and do it right because they are watching! It was not a painful process at all. For a few weeks, I had some stitching. At one of my regular doctor's visits, I was all set with one snip. I was in the viable stage now, passed my 26 weeks. Hannah decided to wait until the date given to her.

Our Royal Baby Shower

So many family and friends were elated for us. When I was about seven months pregnant, there was a baby shower to celebrate baby Hannah's arrival. Upstairs in Christina Cultural Arts Center, where I worked as a Family Services Coordinator, the tables were set, the games were played, there was great food, and lots of friends filled two long tables and the surrounding floor with gifts. We had diapers and pull-ups to last us until she was potty trained. We had to take several trips and multiple cars to drop everything off to our house when the party was over. Her hot pink walls, hot pink carpet, and Snow White furniture with white lace curtains in her bow window, turned into a baby hub. It took days to sort through and organize 0-3 months to 36-months sections in the drawer and in her closet, and I had to be creative. The letters H.A.N.N.A.H. were hanging on her wall over her changing table. Under her letters was a hot pink glove with a white softball. Her daddy, who was a shortstop, was so proud to see his little girl light up and reach for the catcher's mitt and ball.

Positioning Ourselves for the Promise

At a wedding, I sang the same song I sang down the aisle at my wedding. During the reception, I went to the bathroom because I felt this weird discharge. My then husband was standing outside the bathroom and asked if I was okay. We went to the dance floor to congratulate the bride and the groom and told them that we were having a baby on their wedding day. Everybody celebrated! We were excited and nervous at the same time, but it turned out to be a false alarm. It was just the plug. What is a plug? A gooey cord?

They monitored me overnight. The following week we celebrated another friend. I could feel my body shifting. Something different was taking place. Listen to your body. When I got home, I took a picture with my huge belly. That night was the last night of laying on my side. At about three in the morning, I knew it was time to wash up. We arrived at Christiana close to five in the morning. The pains grew stronger at noon. I requested oxygen to help relieve the anguish, and it worked significantly!

Around 3 p.m. I said, "Where is my epidural!? Lord, I want to be a big girl. I don't want any drugs! This hurts!" They told me don't wait too late to request it, because at some point they will not be able to help me. Just in time, the generals walked in. My mother and Pastor Phil were there to help me pray, calm me down, and line my body up to welcome Hannah in this world. Pastor Phil left my room to visit someone else in the hospital because it was almost my time. Pastor Sylvia Davenport came in his place. She and my mother were my strength. Thank you, Lord for sending my help! It was 5 p.m., then 7 p.m. *Why does this take so long? I have never ever heard of a baby falling asleep during labor.*

They told me not to push or bear down until they tell me because the epidural drugs numbed me up. I could still feel the pain by the way. Every time they got excited, "We see her hair! Head is pushing down! Oh, never mind." *Nevermind!?! What do you mean, nevermind?*

"She went back up."

"What!?" She actually did this about four times before she came out. Hannah was letting us all know she wanted to sleep a little longer. To this day, she doesn't mind extra sleep. I could tell this was Pastor Sylvia's first time seeing a birth on the other side. She was so squeamish. It was a good story to share later.

My mother kept speaking softly to Hannah saying, "Come on baby, come to Grandma. Hannah, Grandma wants to see you, my baby." This little girl obeyed grandma's soft tone and began to help me bear down. It took a long time to push, but she finally made it to fulfill her purpose.

I thank God with all of my heart for allowing my grandmother Inez to see my first-born weeks before she transitioned to glory. Hannah Hephzibah means God's grace and favor on us and His delight is in her. She truly has brought great joy to us all.

As a small child, Hannah's infectious personality changed the atmosphere of any room she walked in. She would greet everyone, smile, ask questions, and show concern for them. At an early age, she would prophesy to people what thus saith the Lord. I don't think she would even know what she was saying at the time. Yet, people would stop to listen intently. I know that the promises of God are yes and Amen.

I could go on and on about so many things I am very proud of Hannah for. Before creating her portfolio for schools, I compiled events and timelines that have shaped her personality through the years. At Kuumba Academy, Hannah took part in two summer programs that she enjoyed. One was Kid Chef, a cooking class for youth. The other was the Urban Bike Project, where she learned how to fix bicycles from beginning to end. I noticed she was a hands-on learner–show her once and let her create. Kuumba has also pulled out her theatrical talents. She told me she was just an extra in the musical production Aladdin Jr., but I was amazed to see her in almost every scene, up front shining like, "This is my shot!"

I was in tears from the magic being created. My love was never into sports until Kuumba prepared them for the 5K run, "Girls on the Run." Between that and Kuumba's Girl Scouts, Hannah has shown me her entrepreneurial skills even at an early age. Girl Scouts taught her to crochet, sell cookies, network, and work well with other girls to reach a common goal. Their rewards were trips to Kings Dominion, the movies, and basketball games in Philadelphia, which piqued Hannah's interests. I later transferred her to Warner Elementary School where she remained on the honor roll. As a result, Hannah gained a scholarship to receive a new guitar and lessons thanks to Ellen Salcedo. We created a special friendship with Ellen. Hannah had the opportunity to sing and play on a backyard stage with her, and I look forward to more of those special moments in time. We have yet to see what astounding being she will become. She is a Communications Arts major at Cab Calloway doing great things in graphic design, so it's clear that creating is natural for her. I watch how her sensitivity still carries the mantle of creating in the Spirit. At her young age, she is powerful; she envisions and then creates. Hannah now has her eye on San Francisco Institute of Art. Lord, You have always spoiled her and answered her prayers. Thank you in advance! At the age of 14, she is off to a great start owning her own graphic design business. Her bright future says Hannah, Graphic Designer. She will always be my baby.

Hadassah Halel

Strength of a Myrtle Tree
Queen Esther, originally named Hadassah, put all her faith in God.
Her faith was a symbol of recovery and establishment of God's promises

Hannah was only two years old. I was about 12-14 weeks, when I found out I was with child again. Boy, for someone who didn't get along with her husband, I sure stayed pregnant for about four years in a row on bed rest. I made the mistake of allowing what the doctor said about my past to get a cerclage for Hadassah, and this time they put me to sleep to do the procedure. I should have never allowed that. Nothing was different so why did I need anesthesia? Nevertheless, I did, and that pregnancy came with a cesarean section.

During the delivery, although I had an epidural, I could feel the blade cutting me open. Next, I felt the weird feeling of my skin separating. Shortly after, I became extremely cold. My body started to shiver uncontrollably. It was puzzling that they could clearly see me shaking terribly but did nothing. I continued to ask for a heating blanket to cover my top half. Finally, they obliged and covered me up. It took a while for my body to calm down and regulate. Then it happened, behind that blue cloth that shielded us from the gore, came a beautiful cry. She had a strong voice. I could only look over at the table while they cleaned her up. Hadassah is her name. My very own

Pocahontas mocha doll baby looked so serious at me as if to say, "You got me?" She cried so much!

I didn't realize that the engorgement wasn't giving her ample supply. My breasts were full, but milk was not coming out for her to drink. I was very weak and was trying to build my strength back up to walk and even hold my baby. One time, I was so scared I thought I was going to drop her. I had to put pillows up on the rail to support us. Soon, the doctors told me I had a fever in the incision. I was not comfortable with all the gauze packing strips they were pushing in me to soak up whatever was coming out, and I had enough. I wanted to go home. They explained that if they discharged me and I became sick from the fever, I would have to be readmitted without my newborn, so I thought, "Never mind, I'll stay."

They never told me about the process to heal from a cesarean. The nurse had to come to my home to monitor the fever in my incision. She was packing the gauze strips between my stitches.

So, I asked, "How am I to heal and close up the incision if I am constantly getting gauze packed in?" There comes a time when you pray and trust God, our healer.

Days after my cesarean, we were moving. Though my body was far from healed, I was boxing and helping with the storage unit prep and getting the moving truck. Ugh! How strong do I have to be to push my way through a situation? Right now, I need some help! Thank God my mother, Ruth Church, in New Castle, my father, Giles Campbell, came on Amtrak from South Carolina, and my sister, KayVersa, drove from Virginia to be my strong support system.

I had to nurse a newborn and care for a three-year-old, because Curt didn't know he had diabetes and high blood pressure. He was so weak. The week I went back to work, he ended up in the hospital with sugar levels at 1110. The doctors said he should have been in a diabetic coma. Things that I don't want to mention began to escalate. Those drugs told me, "You married it, deal with it." At that point, I laid aside what the Bible said on divorce. I made a choice in that instant to file for divorce so my girls could live a healthy life. Even when I was carrying Hadassah, I made a conscious decision to have these girls for myself. We moved in with sister Brenda, a church member, during a snowstorm trying to figure out how to move forward, despite the fact that we didn't like each other. Hannah instantly rebelled after Hadassah was born.

She looked around like, "Who is this baby in my place? Take her back! And where is my daddy?" It got real. I never imagined being a single mother. I never imagined that a Christian would betray us for drugs! *I thought I heard You plainly Lord that this was my husband. Why are You allowing this to happen?* Now, I know the difference between did *God* say or did *I* say.

After church one day, we smiled and greeted one another, so high from the Word of God. Pastor Phil would teach us and break that Word down so even the children left with understanding. Routinely, I was welcomed with excitement by two young, single mothers. We'd take time to fellowship after church, sharing our week, and our children's stories.

One of them said, "Where is your husband, we haven't seen him lately?" I told them we got a divorce. The conversations and smiles turned grim. It was so quiet. In that instant, they cried.

I said, "Oh no, what happened?"

They said, "We're sorry! It's like you told us someone died. We looked up to you two. You two were our role models for marriage." *Oh my God, what just happened?* My heart became heavy because I understood the covenant was not just for our children, but others around us. They were right. The moment I made up in my mind to file for divorce, felt like a death. The enemy surely stole that one, *but my God will restore and recover all!*

During uncertain times, look at your children. You will change your perspective every time.

My baby girl is truly strong like the meaning of her name. She is grounded, brave, and adventurous. Hadassah has a lot of bounce back! She understands differently. She is stronger at dealing with situations. Perhaps it's because all she has known is one parent. Unfortunately, I had to make many adjustments with two small children and an average income. Through it all, God blessed us with a house of our own. My girls have new space to play and an environment of their own. This is our peaceful haven. Just a few summers in, we experienced a summer with no lights. These little girls turned the experience into campfire games with tents and flashlights. We had dinner in candlelight. They called it dinner and a movie. I would have the laptop on with a good family film. While they were enjoying whatever creation formed in their minds, I was internally sobbing. When the battery died on the laptop, that meant it was bedtime. Their imaginations and creativity shielded them from what was really going on. I felt so bad for putting them in that position. It is not easy for a single mother to compromise paying some bills and letting others get behind.

There was a time when Dassah had a kindergarten graduation, and no relatives came. To this day, I can't forgive myself. I felt a tug of war between keeping my job or attending my baby's big day. I truly wished my family treated my children with some level of importance. To them it was just a kindergarten graduation. She received so many awards, I even received awards and was not present to celebrate her or receive them. She cried profusely when I did arrive. I held her tight and realized nothing could ever replace this day. You cannot buy gifts to make up for that hurt and pain, but we went to the mall to finally get that Build-A-Bear she always wanted. Still nothing could ever take the place of your presence to celebrate the amazing child she is.

We were in transition with two used cars breaking down, and again I internally cried out to God. Lord, it was too hot to have my queens out there. I had to take two buses which took over an hour more than a car ride would have. Whether it was too hot or freezing cold with ice on the ground, I hated putting my precious jewels in dire situations. Remember, that was my perspective. Once again, Hannah and Hadassah turned the lack of transportation to including me in hand games while waiting for the bus. They would race to each corner giggling. They enjoyed watching unusual people and getting snacks from the corner store. Mothers always want the absolute best for their children. Young people have a way of helping you enjoy the moment.

I noticed that Hadassah would always watch Hannah and learn what to do and what not to do. While I was helping Hannah with her homework, little Dassah would shout the answer. That little lady is a thinker and a quick learner. She has stayed on the honor roll with the exception of two marking periods. She observes her surroundings accordingly. I feel special to have Hadassah add to the joy Hannah has brought me. They balance one another out, and their different personalities complement each other. Like her middle name, Halel, she is a worshipper. Dassah was the smallest praise dancer in Ezion Fair Baptist dance ministry. When she was in front of the church with many others, her full focus was glorifying God through dance. The church was blessed by her poise and precision at the age of 3-4 years old. She recognizes when God is in the midst. At times, she has dreams that have come to reality. If I broke a spiritual fast when I felt vertigo, Dassah would get away from me and stay on course. The times I'd go out in the community to feed the hungry, Hadassah never hesitated to join me.

Hannah might say at times that Hadassah is an annoying little sister with nails. The honest feelings kick in when Dassah visits her friend.

Hannah says, "Mom I miss her. When is Dassah coming home?" If Dassah is in another room, then Hannah says she is cute, joyful, and funny.

Hadassah's joy for "Girls on the Run" helped shape her second-place win at the Turkey Trot. She also gained second place with the track team X-pectations.

At Cab Calloway School of the Arts, she majors in Communication Arts, and she is still developing a love for the piano. I love how she walks up to the piano singing and playing worship songs. I join in and harmonize what is in her spirit.

For some reason, Hadassah desires to go to University of Georgia to perfect her gymnastics abilities. I do not understand a career in gymnastics, but it is my responsibility to help her keep focused on her dreams.

My Godchildren

I have two goddaughters and two godsons. Quiera and Quintaya (TayTay) were my first bonus blessings before I had children of my own. I was able to develop a relationship until I got married and lost Emmanuel and Eden. It wasn't fair to them that I lost myself. I am grateful that Quiera still allows a space for me to reach out and spend time with her. There is a mature love connection we share now. I missed a lot of her teenage years.

Valentines' Day 2021, we were having such a great time at Bowlerama. My girls understood when Quiera and I stopped the game for a moment to just talk. She had been trying to process and push through losing several loved ones back-to-back. I could understand her heart since Emmanuel and Eden transitioned in the same year. We both understood that God never makes mistakes. Although we had already been faced with tragedy, we both chose to live and not die in our process. We both chose to create the best versions of ourselves. God will complete a good work in us after all. We caught up about topics like relationships and how she is a queen, to tattoos, to our next quality time together. I am so appreciative of moments like these.

My girls love their god brother, Noah Quintell, so much! We just met baby Isaiah, but they want me to give them brothers from my womb. I remind them I don't have a husband, and that I am close to 50 (sounds like Sara a little). Lord help their understanding. At my age, it's time to embrace God brothers and/or foster brothers. I told them that through their God brothers, my two lost children are restored. It didn't quite come the way I thought, but all of my children are promises manifested. I know that the Lord will also recover the right relationship: the right husband for me and a bonus dad for them. When Meemom Michelle came to ask me to be Noah's godmother, he leaned in from his car seat, looked up at me with such a look, like "You know you want to." I knew we were connected, so I said yes! I later found out that Noah and Emmanuel's birthdays were two days apart, both in March. How special and significant is that! Restoration!

The Doctors do not have the final say.
Yes, at 33 and 36 years old, God reversed the narrative.
I became Hannah and Hadassah's mommy. God, You Are faithful!

I am grateful and blessed to see my children grow up to be the promises that God gave me years ago. I had hoped I was successfully married showing these queens what it's like to be treated as the precious jewels they are. God still truly smiles on me, and so do Emmanuel and Eden. I still keep them in a perfect place in my heart. I sometimes feel them joining conversations and in the laughter that I share with Hannah and Hadassah. It is well with my soul.

In the midst of the pandemic, I am enjoying my family like never before. During this time, we have bonded more; we are not so busy with outside agendas and there's so much laughter.

Periodically my girls would say, "Mom what would you do if you had all four of us here acting up?"

I would say, "Oh Lord," with a big smile because I feel their presence at times. We are at peace. I am in a good space.

Every year on the anniversary of my son and daughter's passing, I take off from work because the children that I work with are about their age. I would wonder what they would be doing if they had been here. Two years ago, I didn't take off; I went to lunch and everything was great. It was a beautiful day, but I found myself crying in my car out of nowhere.

"Wow, I thought I was over this," I thought. I stayed in the car as long as I could, dried my eyes, and when I went back in for my lunch, the children immediately felt something was wrong. I cried again in the classroom, and all the children surrounded me with hugs and love. *What is going on? This was close to 15 years ago! What is wrong with me?* That was 2019. In March 2020, I was healed, and I no longer felt empty.

This assignment was designed to help me heal properly. It is now up to me to keep Quiera, Tay Tay, Hannah, Hadassah, Noah, and Isaiah surrounded in God's purpose.

Writing has truly been therapeutic. I do realize I need to write more or speak with a therapist to make sure I am not suppressing my feelings towards leaving my children at the hospital. I'm relieving myself of the *should haves* and *could haves*. God is definitely a restorer, a healer, and a deliverer, and I love Him so much for comforting me.

It is Wednesday, March 3rd, 2021. It feels like the first sign of Spring, and it's a new season. I am smiling and honestly feeling well. God is truly faithful!

"through whom we have gained access by faith into this grace in which we now stand. And we boast in the hope of the glory of God. Not only so, but we also glory in our sufferings, because we know that suffering produces perseverance; perseverance, character; and character, hope." Romans 5:2-4

If you have lost children and have not had any more, I pray that you trust God, and he will restore.

About *Selara*

Selara Gatewood, of Brooklyn (Crown Heights), New York is a mother of two wonderful and beautiful daughters, Hannah and Hadassah, and is a Special Education Paraeducator. Selara continues to develop minds with her tutoring group, Metanoia Tutors business. She has many years in Banking and before that she was a Retail Lead Manager at Sears Prices Corner for many years. She also enjoyed helping others as a Family Services Coordinator, connecting families to resources in the community. She has traveled to places such as India, Mexico, Jamaica and Haiti. Her self-care is enjoying worship music because it creates her safe space and a peaceful haven for her to completely rest and trust in God.

Thank You Ms. Eleanor Brown for your Wishes, Love, Blessings, Encouragement Kindness + Support.
I pray you are Blessed By the Many Stories for God's Glory.

Dear Diary:

"The Shift…"

PAIN TO POWER
Shané Darby

I cringe at the thought of my daughter's dating, having sex, and even having a heart break one day, but I know it is inevitable. If I were to imagine anyone being with my daughters, I want them to be a Black person who loves them unconditionally, supports them in their goals in life, allows room for individuality, and who balances them and makes them feel at ease in loving, communicating, and negotiating. One thing I understand about dating and relationships is that an individual can be highly impacted by what relationships they saw their parents navigating in.

My parents met in college. My mom got pregnant with me and dropped out of school. My biological father also dropped out of school, married my mother, joined the military, and they moved to Germany. I actually have no declarative memory of Germany; my earliest memory of them is actually living in Oklahoma. I can't recall any good memories of them together. I remember constant arguing, cussing, yelling, and fighting between them. I remember waking up from my sleep crying and frightened by the sight of my parents fighting. I never witnessed them hugging, kissing, or showing affection or love towards each other. They ended in a terrible divorce as I was starting Kindergarten in Delaware.

Twelve years later, I ended up in an abusive relationship. This boy was four years older than me, and I was captivated by his smooth dark skin, wavy hair, and bright smile. The abuse built up and it got worse. After prom night, we went to his house, he stripped me ass naked, and dragged me up the steps because he believed that I was cheating on him with one of my close guy friends. No one was around. At the time, I didn't realize it was wrong. I had recently found out I was pregnant, and he knew. I wanted him to be the father of my child. After that, I stayed at his house still and had sex with this boy.

I ended up having three girls with him over a 10-year span, my first when I was 19 years old, and the other two when I was 26 and 27 years old. During all three pregnancies, I experienced physical, mental, and verbal abuse. I was punched in the stomach and kicked several times, my hair was pulled, I was smacked in the face, called a bitch and every other name under the sun, discouraged from any progress I wanted to make in life, and more.

That first pregnancy made a huge difference. He was incarcerated the summer I graduated from high school. I went off to college and that whole four years I still held on to wanting this man in my life. I sent him money on the regular and wrote letters weekly. When he was incarcerated in New Jersey, I visited weekly up until he was transferred to a prison in Virginia. I visited him once when he was in Virginia because I could not afford to visit him more frequently. When he was released from prison, I was starting my master's program in Philadelphia. One year later, the physical and mental abuse resumed, and I became pregnant with my second child. At the time, I was living on campus in college, so I hustled and got a place.

My children's father was absent, and we were on and off. I was exhausted and depressed. I was emotionally, mentally, and physically abused. Within two years, I lost a home due to a fire, lived in a hotel with my children, I got pregnant again, totaled a brand-new car, was hospitalized for a week due to a cyst eruption, and my uncle died.

When I burned down the kitchen in my home, it was because I fell asleep boiling bottles. Afterwards, I lived in a hotel until I got a new apartment a few months later. I found out I was pregnant again, but I did not want to be pregnant. I did not want another child, especially with my children's father. I knew that this was a toxic, unhealthy situation, but I could not break away from him. When times were good, they were great. I held on to the potential of him doing better and him treating me better. I hid my pain and hurt, covering it up and pushing on.

As my family was growing, I purchased a brand-new truck. Not even a year after buying it, I totaled the truck. I fell asleep driving on my way to the hospital with my baby daughter. I hit a car, a person, and a mailbox. After a few days in the hospital, I came home still in so much pain. I had to return to work the following day. Everyday my movement was getting slower and slower. I could barely walk. I was having sharp pains and pressure in my stomach. I remember sitting in my cubicle, popping pain medication to make it through the day. My life did not stop; picking up and dropping off the children and our evening routine continued as usual, and I was trying to keep it all together.

My children's father would not help me, and I did not feel confident in being able to ask for help from my family. By the end of that week, I laid on the bed exhausted. I heard my baby daughter crying, but I could not move. My oldest daughter asked what was for dinner, and I could barely respond back to her. She ended up calling my mom, letting her know something was not right with her mother.

I went to the ER and was admitted for a ruptured ovarian cyst. I received IV pain medication and antibiotics to fight the infection in my body. As I laid there in my own thoughts, I realized my body was speaking to me, telling me it was overstressed, overworked, and exhausted! If I did not come to the hospital, I could have died.

My mind wondered for a week. I began to do a lot of reflecting. I cried a lot. I talked out loud to myself. I had thoughts about not being alive anymore. I would ask for pain medication just to go back to sleep, but my dreams did not spare me from my thoughts; I had vivid dreams and nightmares that gave me revelations about my past, present, and future.

By the end of the week, I was released from the hospital with a sense of calmness and relief, and I felt refreshed. I returned to work the following day and resumed my regular routine with the children. However, within a few days, I got the news my uncle died.

My uncle was in my life since the age of five. My uncle was a very wise and intellectual person; he would recommend books like *Isis Paper* and *They Came Before Columbus* for me to read, which made an impact on my identity and who I am today. I am a naturally born knowledge seeker. We had discussions about culture, boys, history, death, and life. He would use phrases like "Black queen," would explain the benefits of having melanin, and was passionate about Black history, culture, and current issues. He would be the loudest and the proudest of the accomplishments of his loved ones. He was friendly and well-liked by most people.

When I got pregnant with my oldest daughter in high school, I spent a lot of time at my baby father's house while he was incarcerated. My family sent my uncle, knowing our close relationship, and believed he could talk me into getting an abortion. When I walked outside to see my uncle, I gave him a look. From that look, he knew I was about to turn right back around to go inside. I did not want to hear anything from anybody; my decision was final. He knew I was going to keep my daughter and there was not much persuading he could do, but he did sit down on that stoop with me and talked to me for a few hours about some of his life decisions and so much more. I will never forget those conversations with him! This was a norm.

I was devastated at the news of his death. I cried not just for him, but for me. I felt a darkness and a blankness in my thoughts and feelings. I was depleted. I was not sure how much more I could take. I was depressed. I miss him dearly and I am glad that I was able to connect with him during this life.

As my children's dad and I did our normal "two-step" of arguing and fighting each other, our daughters watched, screamed, and cried in fear, so I knew this had to end. I flashed back to myself as a child witnessing the abuse my father put my mother through, and my heart broke as I realized my daughters were me. I had to break this cycle and release. I felt a shift coming.

I had to release

I had to release generational trauma.
I had to release a dysfunctional relationship.
I had to release toxic energy.
I had to release low vibrating thoughts.
I had to release the "strong Black woman" narrative.
I had to release low self-esteem.
I had to release dysregulation of emotions.
I had to release daddy issues.
I had to release mommy issues.
I had to release abandonment issues.
I had to release anger.
I had to release self-doubt.
I had to release masculine energy.
I had to release chaos.
I had to release confusion.
I had to release feeling mentally stagnant.
I had to release fear of failure.
I had to release fear of the unknown.
I had to release distractions.

I had to restore. I had to replenish. I realized that embracing categories such as the "strong Black woman" was an insult to my divinity. I began a journey. I started to visualize this release, and I started to re-discover my why. I started to become selfish about loving and caring for me. I embraced my divinity. I stood firm.

Self-reflection was central. I started becoming more in tune with my emotions and even acknowledging them. I wanted to scream, "*I am a human, I have feelings, I am not conforming, I am vulnerable!*" I started to sit with myself once a month to reflect. I needed to nurture the little girl inside of me. I wanted to love myself, find myself, and protect my daughters.

I realized I overcame a lot. In a short timeframe, I experienced trauma and grief back-to-back. I never took time to reflect and to heal. I grew up in a house where feelings were not discussed. I was taught to keep going. I did not have proper coping skills. I knew that I wanted my daughters to have the coping skills to deal with life's challenges, so I began therapy sessions.

Moreover, I started to take responsibility for my own actions and emotions in the past and the present. I started to be intentional in my actions with myself and others, especially my children. I wanted to love myself. I created boundaries with everyone in my life. My motto became *"I do not care who I lose today. I have shit to do."* If it did not align with my why, my purpose, and my healing, I decided how I would engage. Even with people I loved, I had to decide to choose me. In my self-reflection, I declared that I would determine my future. I had gratitude for the now but was excited for the future.

Surrounding myself with positive, like-minded, or inspiring people was my next step. I began to network and just put myself in rooms. I specifically knew I wanted a network of Black women that could provide me with love, support, and genuine friendship.

Call me the "Goal Executer" because over the last two years, I have accomplished every goal I visualized. As a natural fighter, a grinder, and hustler, I dreamt big, and I was not afraid to fail. I began to work hard to accomplish what I visualized. I tapped into my energy and my greatness. I had to fight through self-doubt and outside voices telling me certain things were not possible.

Through these new lenses of just being, I started to see the beauty of the world. I was relieved of stress and understood how to maintain stress that existed. I started to seek knowledge. I explored new things such as meditation, spirituality, yoga, etc.

I feel at peace and relaxed, like a huge weight was lifted off my body and mind. Blessings began to overflow, and I knew it was okay to be free.

I now feel like my true, authentic, and raw self.

About *Shané Darby*

Shané is a proud mother of three girls, Saniyah, Samirah, and Skai. She was born and raised in Wilmington and is a proud descendant of Black Immigrants and American Enslaved Black people (ADOS). She is the founder of Black Mothers In Power, a non-profit focused on addressing Black maternal healthcare through the state of Delaware. She is passionate about Black maternal healthcare and recently became trained as a postpartum doula. Shané is also a mental health counselor working closely with children in Wilmington who have experienced trauma. She also serves as the 2nd District Councilperson for Wilmington and a paralegal in the Army National Guard.

Dear Diary:

"Note to self: Stop taking everything so personal."

YOU MATTER
Sunshine

"Sticks and stones can break my bones, but names/words will never hurt me."

This statement is one of the biggest lies ever told. Words have power and life. Growing up, I was always "plump." I got teased a lot because of my size. I got called out of my name because of my size. I was chosen last because of my size. I had crushes on boys who ignored me because of my size. Hearing and experiencing those things as a child going into my teen years, I thought I was too big to wear pants and would only wear skirts and dresses. As an adolescent I can remember being with my middle big sister, and guys that she knew would speak to me. Then I would hear her say, "Hey! That's my baby sister, (insert a couple of choice words)!" I'm certain they said some inappropriate things to cause her to react like that. Then I would hear some of the ladies at church say, "She's cute and shapely. She's just a little chubby." You see, I was as they say, "Plump like a roast and thicker than most." I didn't know what I had. No wonder my sister's vocabulary would change when those guys said stuff. Fast forward. I'm now a teenager.

Let's go shopping!

Ooooh! I like this! Nice!

Whomp, whomp!

I can't fit it. I'm too big. The clothes in the "chubby" section look like something a grandmom would wear. And here I am, feeling bad about myself again.

Time

How much does time cost? Have you ever wanted nothing but to just spend a little bit of time with someone?

"Now is not a good time."

We're spending time together. We're having a great time, then I don't see you until the next day. Where did you go? It's a new day. Here's another chance at spending time together. Now I see you. Now I don't. Where did you go this time? I guess we'll try again at another time.

"Let's spend some time together."

Oh yeah! I am so excited!

It's the same cycle.

Time has passed and I'm asked again, "Can we spend some time together?"

No thank you. I don't want to. Cue the raised wall for protection. Years have passed. A major accomplishment is about to happen in my life, and I want you there to celebrate with me. It cost nothing but "time." I get the answer, "I can't make it. I have church," And the wall goes back up again. Every time I start letting the wall down, it feels like I'm one of the word bubbles in a batman and robin cartoon!

Smack! Bang! Kaboom! Kersplat!

I am sick of it!

It's funny how the tables turn. Now you want to spend time with me.

I forgive you.

I love you.

I respect you, but I'm scared to let the wall down for fear of being hurt yet again. Getting hurt, hurts and I choose to not be hurt again.

You make yourself available for folk. You stop, drop, and roll to accommodate them and it's not reciprocated. You get invited to a friend or family event just days before it happens while everyone else has been talking about if for a while. *What am I, an afterthought? Oh, I get it. You already paid and don't want to lose out on that ticket. So now I'm invited?*

Wow! Or you simply find out after the fact when folk are talking about the grand time they had. You smile on the outside while on the inside if feels like someone is pouring alcohol onto an open wound. Oh well, I was always told that I was "a square" anyway. Could it be because I danced to my own beat? Or perhaps, because I didn't do or wasn't into what everyone else was into? Shrug and square your shoulders girl! Be like a duck and let it roll off of your back!

So what?!

You try with all your might to do this, but guess what?

It still hurts.

"Shut up! You sound dumb! Nobody wants to hear what you have to say!" We never get tired of each other. We always talked. I loved you so that if you said the sky is purple with orange stripes and pink polka dots, I would have believed you. We shared our inner most secrets with each other, things that other people said or did to us that we didn't like and how it made us feel less than.

BRRRR! It's getting cold! What's going on?

The sun isn't shining as bright anymore. Things are cloudy.

Hello?

Where are you?

Oh, there you are! Wait a minute! It's you, but it's not you. You look like you. Something is strange. You're not acting like you. Can we talk? I'm airing my feelings like we use to do. Wait! How did this become my fault? I just wanted to talk about how you were beginning to make me feel bad. I'm not perfect, but what have I done to you? What happened to us sitting and talking for hours? What happened to our "intense" discussions where we talked until everything was ironed out? Can we talk?

"Shut up! You sound so dumb!"

I grow quiet. I try to begin a conversation again only to have you use some of the hurtful things I shared with you early on against me. *Ouch!* We're in the presence of other people. I try to engage in the conversation then I hear a familiar voice say, "You sound so dumb! Just be quiet! Nobody wants to hear that! Say something else dumb!

Just dumb!" Now I'm quiet. I don't say anything. I don't initiate conversations anymore. I don't want to feel dumb or be called dumb again. I just smile. I have great conversations in my head. I'm not cut off. I can say whatever I want. I talk a little around other people, but not too much, because you know, I don't want to sound or feel dumb.

Aren't you tired of this?

Yes!

Aren't you tired of feeling like a door mat?

Yes!

Love me or leave me alone! I'm tired of this! Stand up for yourself, girl! I grew good and tired of being made to feel less than, or like I wasn't smart or good enough. I began to speak up for myself. Those great conversations that I was having in my head became audible for others to hear. I demand and command respect. You *will not* speak to me that way! You *will not* treat me any kind of way! I made a decision. Deuce's! I'm out!

I am *free*! I speak more now. At times I can be very talkative and will even laugh out loud! I find myself thinking before I speak so that I don't sound, you know, dumb. Guess what? People actually want to hear what I have to say! I'm still hesitant at times. I have a lot of love in my heart and don't mind sharing it. I love seeing people smile and at times I'm the guilty party to cause that to happen intentionally and unintentionally. I love giving compliments and encouraging words. Sometimes it's hard for me to receive compliments for the positive things that I do, but I'm getting better with that. One day I was having a conversation with my sister/friend. We were talking about how our bubbly and caring personalities affect people we come in contact with. This made me think about every job that I have had in my adult life. I remembered that I was given the nick name "Sunshine" at every job!

Girl, what are you doing? Be contagious and spread love, joy, and peace! I want to share this with you and encourage you as I encourage myself.

Proverbs 18:20-21 Message

"Words satisfy the mind as much as fruit does the stomach; good talk is as gratifying as a good harvest. Words kill, words give life; they're either poison or fruit...you choose."

Psalm 139:14-15 TPT

"I thank you, God, for making me so mysteriously complex! Everything you do is marvelously breathtaking. It simply amazes me to think about it! How thoroughly you know me, Lord! You even formed every bone in my body when you created me in the secret place, carefully and skillfully shaping me from nothing to something."

Jeremiah 29:11 KJV

"For I know the thoughts that I think toward you, saith the Lord, thoughts of peace, and not of evil, to give you an expected end."

Proverbs 12:18 TPT

"Reckless words are like the thrusts of a sword, cutting remarks meant to stab and to hurt. But the words of the wise soothe and heal."

Proverbs 16:24 TPT

"Nothing is more appealing than speaking beautiful, life giving words. For they release sweetness to our souls and inner healing to our spirits."

Guess what? *I matter and so do you.* Sunshine, signing off.

About *Sunshine*

Sunshine, born Shariece Beecham, is honored to be the mother of a niece/daughter, son, daughter, daughter-in-love, four grandboys and one grandgirl. They are all her favorites! She loves spending time with her family and creating memories. She has been an Early Childhood Educator for 30 years and is passionate about the lives she gets to make a difference in on a daily basis. It brings her great joy to watch and help children discover and explore their world. It is her prayer that as you read her words, that you are encouraged, and uplifted. *You matter.*

Dear Diary:

"Once again, he met me right where I needed Him to!"

TABITHA, THE BARREN ONE
Tammy Moody

Once there was a little girl named Tabitha who had so many dreams and aspirations of being a mother. Her bedroom was her sanctuary of peace and harmony and she could be found reading books and telling stories to her dolls. These were no ordinary dolls; they were always wearing the finest dresses. The little girl would always tell her dolls how much they were loved, and that they would grow up to be strong and ambitious women. Then, there was the conversation on the importance of education with goals to not only attend college but finish.

The little girl would be lost for days in her room, talking and reading to these beautiful caramel and chocolate dolls. Then, there would be a knock on the door.

"Oh, come on downstairs and get something to eat."

"Awe, Mom! can't I just eat in my room?"

Mother responded, "No!"

"Awe, Mom come on!"

With a stern voice, mother said, "Listen, we eat dinner every night at the table."

The little girl pleaded with her mother, "I am eating with my children."

Mother was now beside herself. "Chile, you ain't even old enough to have no children!"

Gasping for air, the little girl said, "Mom!"

So, the little girl, respecting her mother's wishes, retreated down the stairs to the first floor of the two-story home to have dinner at the table with her human family, leaving her dolls in her bedroom. There was always conversation at the dinner table discussing the day's events, but it could get crazy, as Daddy was no longer with them. Daddy died when the little girl was two years old. The absence of Daddy made the dinner table with the four chairs, place setting of dinnerware, and the evening's prepared meal seem empty. Watching Momma moving around the kitchen and the house gave the little girl a sense of safety, because Momma was her provider. Momma was involved in relationships that didn't fit her mold of Daddy. Some of the men could be father figures, but the little girl had no confidence that any of the men could reach the high standard of "Daddy." Deep down inside, the little girl needed and wanted a Daddy at the dinner table every night.

In the little girl's neighborhood, there was a boy named Darryl who was very popular with all the kids, and the little girl was also popular with her friends. At the age of 10 years old, the little girl and Darryl locked eyes on each other. Not much came out of the look other than an innocent game of tiddlywinks with an occasional glance of "I see you too."

At age 11, the little girl, now in her pubescent age, began having certain thoughts about Darryl, but she didn't want to get embarrassed in front of Darryl. You see, Darryl was liked by all the girls. She thought if she prepared herself for Darryl, he wouldn't laugh at her if she didn't know what she was doing. Wow, such things for an 11-year-old to be thinking about. She never told anyone her thoughts except her favorite uncle. One day, she reached out to the favorite uncle who all the kids liked because there were no rules or boundaries. She asked him could he help her. On one particular day, she stopped by her uncle's house in route to school.

He asked, "Are you scared?" as she walked in the door.

Although she was nervous as heck, she said, "No," then replied, "A little."

He said, "We don't have to if you don't want to." The little girl didn't want Darryl to tease her about not knowing what to do, so she said, "I'm ok." Her uncle said he had a warm bath for her to relax in.

The little girl asked if he had anything else, and he gave her a joint and some wine. After the bath, she laid in the bed. He began to touch her. It was the first time and it hurt down there, but she never told a soul. She wasn't even all that eager to have Darryl like her now. She went to school and the new journey began.

She started smoking marijuana and getting in trouble. She was a smart girl but was still seeking something more in her life. She had many other encounters with her uncle, and it was a distorted, dysfunctional relationship. She wanted to be Daddy's princess and her uncle made her feel like she was. She was able to drink and smoke with him. Somewhere along this journey she managed to move away from this encounter and distortion of what love was between a girl and boy.

The little girl, no matter her age, knew she was loved by her mother, but she still yearned for that daddy love. The pubescent experience continued to spiral, and the fantasy dwindled, causing her to fall "in and out" of love. Now, at the age of 18, the little girl yearned for children. She wondered why she had not conceived despite the many times she purposefully had intercourse without protection. Later, at the age of 25, she sought medical advice to address reproductive concerns. In giving her medical history, she remembered when she had pelvic inflammatory disease.

The doctor said, "Yes, that does leave scar tissue, but we have many options to try before ruling out conceiving yourself." She thought she was so in love, and she and her boo went to a specialist. He had his sperm counted and she had dye placed in her to see if it would pass through her ovaries. She prayed and prayed that the dye would pass through. With great sadness, she found out that it didn't. She was very disappointed. That was the first time she didn't feel like a woman, and it would be one of many. She became depressed and her mate at the time didn't understand. She was always searching for someone to love her in her barren condition, and the little girl who found sanctuary in her bedroom reading books and talking to her dolls still had the desire to be a mommy.

Watching her own mother show the love to her and her siblings, the 18-year-old continued to yearn for motherhood. The medical appointments left her wanting to make changes to "relive" a better life along with having a significant other to share the joy with her.

Good love and a Daddy seated at the dinner table every night was still missing. The transition to young adulthood brought many people into the little girl's life—some good, some not so good, and some questionable. Graduating from high school was another rite of passage she was proud of, but along with that came the introduction of drugs. She began smoking cigarettes, which led to trying cocaine and other drugs. Life was spiraling into a place that was foggy, but what was always consistent was the yearning for Daddy to be seated every night at the dinner table.

Changes needed to happen, and the little girl decided to get clean at the age of 21 so she had a better shot of becoming a mother. She thought a relationship based in love would increase the chance of having a baby. No baby came, even with all the medical science of in-vitro and an ovulation calendar. The little girl's life began to change, and she often questioned the how, why, and when. God had another path for her, which included learning and accepting the true meaning of motherhood and bettering herself intellectually. She went on and received her bachelor's degree and then master's degree.

The little girl became godmother to many children, and they became her whole world. The little girl, along with her husband, loved and showered her godchildren with positive experiences and exposure to educational and cultural events. She even parented a godchild for six years because the birth parents had experienced a tragic death of a loved one and were unable to care for the child. The little girl observed her godchild's parents and other family members' dysfunction over the years. The godchild's family only wanted to parent the child when it was convenient for them, placing the child on a mantle to sit quietly until called or if there was monetary gain. The little girl only wanted to love him and raise him to see beyond his circumstances. The opportunity presented itself, and the little girl made sure her godson went to all his doctor's appointments, went to church with her, and was enrolled in a private school.

Then, her heart was ripped from her when the parents found out the child was eligible for social security because of a medical diagnosis and demanded their child be returned home. The little girl prayed over her godson and let him go. A lot of time passed before she could spend quality time with him again. She knew that prayer worked and just kept praying over his life and his parents. She asked God to heal her heart, and she thanked him for the time she had with her godson.

The little girl who could be found in her bedroom reading and talking to her beautifully dressed caramel and chocolate dolls, knew the importance of showing and telling children they are loved. Children need a safe place to be cared for, to laugh, rest and be loved. There are some people that are blessed to give birth to children but place the child on the shelf when they see fit. The little girl had to deal with the devastation and had to learn not to be angry because the birth parents were not aware of the needs of their child. She had to acknowledge that having children for her may look different. She started thinking about adoption and foster care. That would mean teaching the children in her care that they were loved and were special. She thought about the scripture Genesis 9:7 (NHEB): "*Be fruitful and multiply, increase abundantly on the earth and subdue it.*" The revelation came that whatever season she may have with any child, that they are to know God loves them, has a plan for their lives, and there is nothing they could do about it but accept their calling. She wanted to give herself freely with no condition to her love. God was slowly showing the little girl that her path to motherhood was expanding. A mother's job is unconditional with no boundaries.

At the ripe age of 43 years old, the little girl was blessed with the opportunity to co-parent another little boy name DJ. She promised God that she was going to do it right this time. There are children all over the world without parents, and the little girl realized she was here to share her love with them. The little girl learned to become a listening ear and helped other mothers to find their parenting style. She taught her young child that he had multiple people in his village that loved him, and she too had to learn to let go of the fear that her little boy would transition his love to another. It was also important for the little boy to know that Jesus loved him. They would spend days reading, going to church, and declaring God's word over his life.

DJ was a special little boy who had drugs in his system from his birth mother. It pressed on the little girl's heart and mind to make sure that he was afforded all the opportunities possible. As he began school, the little girl noticed that the little boy needed additional services in school, and she advocated for all his needs.

God must have thought the little girl was able to love and raise another. The little girl, now 45 years old, was given the opportunity to raise her godson's daughter. The beautiful caramel brown-skinned baby was in her arms at two months old and never left. The mother and father of the baby were having some challenging times and did not want to put the baby in harm's way. The godson remembered his experiences being raised by his godmother for six years of his life and often said he regrets that his parents did not let him stay. He believed his life would have been different. This did her heart well to hear this.

He said, "Mom, my daughter is better with you." Her heart skipped many beats. Now the little girl had a boy and girl to raise. The little girl remembered walking the floor with SuMyah every night. She had these very bad dreams. She laid on the little girl's bosom and the little girl felt a love like no other. She would pray and read to her many stories from the Bible and tell her she could be anything she put her mind to. The little girl impressed upon her the importance of knowing Jesus for herself.

The children were so wonderful to watch grow up together, and the little girl prayed and declared God's word over their lives. Because both the children had drugs in their system when they were born, the little girl knew that it was only going to be the love of God and stability that would give them the life they deserved.

Parenting for the little girl now looks like being a mom to an 11-year-old son who is taller than her. There was a time that the son found his voice to state, "You are not my Mom." His father, who is seated at the dinner table every night, explained to their young son that God gave him to them. God knew the love and care that he would have in that family. They never wanted him to think that he was unloved by his birth mother–quite the opposite–she loved him enough to let him go. He was happy to know that he was so loved, and he never brought the matter up again. DJ was fully adopted and is now their son! He is a very respectable, loving boy and takes after his father; very quiet, humble, caring, helpful, and very conscious about God.

He often lays his head on the little girl's bosom and says, "Mom, I love you," which seems to be a reoccurring theme in the home.

Now parenting the amazing six-soon-to-be-seven-year-old has been absolutely phenomenal for the little girl. From watching her take her first steps, to climbing out the playpen and highchair, to her saying her first words "dadda and pop pop" and then "mom mom," to her singing and declaring she is a child of the most high King, to her elaborate personality, to her fashion sense, to her quickness to pray for the homeless, to her care for all people of all colors, to her special love for her own skin tone, to her embracing that she is more than a conqueror in Christ Jesus when uncomfortable thoughts or sounds come her way. The little girl is amazed to watch her granddaughter pray and calm herself to be at a place of peace. She has the opportunity to love her birth parents and see them periodically, but she knows where her stability lies.

Imagine having a conversation with a six-year-old that goes something like this.

"Mom! You know I am not dating until I am 45 and finished school."

"Wow! Really?" said Mom. "Why is that?"

"I will be old enough to get married, have kids, and I will have my career like you and Pop Pop."

"I think that is a wonderful start," said Mom as she smiled.

The little girl now sits at the table with her husband and her children. The little girl remembers the empty chair at her dinner table when she was growing up, but now all chairs are filled, not just with a father's presence, but with children's as well.

God has always been sitting at the table letting the little girl know that she was not alone. Being a parent is more than giving birth, it is rolling through the obstacles and challenges that the children experience. It is about being selfless so that the children's needs are met. It is being available when they need someone they trust to listen without judgement. It is about giving your last so that they can have what they need. It is also making those hard decisions for the betterment of their wellbeing. The sacrifice of parenting these two bundles of joy has fulfilled the fantasy of the little girl in her room talking to her caramel and chocolate dolls.

About *Tammy Moody*

Minister Tammy Moody gave her life to Christ as a child and renewed her vow to God in 1989 after years of drug and alcohol abuse, broken relationships, and misguided information. Moody is the owner and founder of God Future & Associates, a faith-based company providing counseling and other services to youth and adults. She received her Bachelor of Science in Human Services with a concentration in Project Development and her master's degree in Human Services with a concentration in Counseling Drug & Alcohol, Family, and Youth. Mrs. Moody also attended Liberty Theological School. Throughout her career, she helped to reunite over 100 children with their mothers and fathers and has assisted over 150 at-risk youth with getting out of the juvenile system. Mrs. Moody is happily married to her Boaz, Chef David Moody. She has the pleasure of raising their (adopted) son and her granddaughter, which brings them so much joy and happiness. She assisted her husband in opening their catering business called 1st Tri Caterers, where they serve the Tri-State region with Godly love and great food! Mrs. Moody is not foreign to hard work and commitment. She believes it takes God to be right there in the center of all you do for you to achieve your desires.

Dear Diary:

"Are you moving out of fear and defeat or confidence and victory?"

COMMITTED TO TRANSFORMATION
Tawana M. Peterson

Ready for the world without fear but harboring regrets, I was 18 years old, entering into life as an independent young adult and able to claim full responsibility for my actions while facing deficits from what life had to offer. I thought I was handling myself decently enough, as most teenage individuals do. I took on the job of being in a full-time relationship at 16 and stayed committed up through my senior year of high school. Hitting areas of indecisiveness and moments of discord, we were coming to a crossroad of great life resolution. I wondered how I really wanted to enter my life as a young adult. *Was I ready to take on this new life following the path that I was taking, or did I need to take a moment to reflect on the things that I was taught?* I was questioning how I was living and considering the God that I wanted to serve.

Amidst of it all, I went to college expecting a child and was determined to make it work. I toiled with the reality and considered the things that I would have to face. I had a secret that no one knew the answer to except the creator of my life. Because of it, I was ashamed, sorrowful, and desired forgiveness for everything that I allowed myself to be a part of. Within that moment of choice, I decided to press reset on my life. I lost that seed through a surgical procedure. It's difficult for me to name it, but for the first time, I'll admit that I had an abortion and I felt as though I would never get that chance at life again. I've read about all the horror stories of lives lost and procedures gone wrong inhibiting conception and the like. I was tormented by my own ideation of what the outcome would be for me as a result of my decision. However, the one saving grace that kept my spirit alive was the fact that I asked God for forgiveness and I had a repentant heart.

Now, at that point, I really gave myself to God in every area of my life. It was as if I had a Saul experience on the road to adulthood. I wasn't condemning my faith, but I certainly wasn't living 100% of the life that I knew I should. I fought through the mental anguish and prayed that God would allow me the chance to live life according to what I said I believed, with the commitment of living life according to the will and plan laid out for me. While torment hovered in my mind, I was presented with the opportunity to, "press reset." I did not fully understand, but in practicing my faith, I encountered the true act of repentance. I had come too far, in my opinion, from where I knew I should have been, and I just wanted to be right. Without truly realizing the magnitude, but trusting in the knowledge of the act, I literally turned from my life's plan and sought the direction of God's plan for my life.

"And he said to them, if any man will come after me, let him deny himself, and take up his cross daily, and follow me. For whosoever will save his life shall lose it: but whosoever will lose his life for my sake, the same shall save it." Luke 9:23-24 (KJV)

I didn't plan my every step, but I had enough faith to believe that I could live the life that God had for me if I became bold enough to surrender. When I found that boldness, those who were meant to be in my life remained, and those who were hindering the process were removed. I was bold enough to confront my concerns and speak of the things that I desired. When I told my significant other at the time that I wanted to change the direction of our relationship—I wanted to practice celibacy until marriage—he couldn't or didn't want to meet me in that space. It was then and there that I found myself in a place of no return. I decided that I had to lose my life as I knew it in order to save it.

As people, we live and grow with understanding that we have to learn to take charge of our actions. We control the direction that we choose to follow when coming to the place of independence. We also often find ourselves taking matters into our own hands and leaning on our own understanding. Why? The answer is clear in my eyes. It was simply thought of as the "coming of age." With this coming of age, it feels like we have so much to prove. The pressure is high and so many eyes are watching your every move. It's a very monumental time, and we are told that the first impression is the most lasting. Sidney Poitier once advised Denzel Washington that, "the first three to five films you make will determine how you are perceived," meaning, make certain that the roles in which you play represent the image that you desire to carry. I took that bit of advice as a life lesson while I sojourned into adulthood, and it's one of the reasons why I chose to go in the direction that I did when I contemplated the furtherance of that pregnancy.

Even though this may be very true and insightful view, what happens when you slip, forget something, or the unforeseen thing happens in the midst of your presentation? The true reality of those mishaps is that they occur for the purpose of providing a lesson to be learned. These moments create opportunity for humility, which is necessary to help us recognize the power of the divine. Without these experiences we could find ourselves operating in a space of illusory superiority, which Psychology Wiki defines as a "cognitive bias that causes people to overestimate their positive qualities and abilities and to underestimate their negative qualities, relative to others." What does this mean? It's necessary to go through moments of challenge and dependency on a source higher than ourselves to recognize that our greatest abilities won't cause us to be overpowered. There is only one who is invincible, and that is God!

I bring this information to the table to shine light on the ease of self-absorption and the necessity of finding balance in how we deal with life and opportunities as a whole. We are living in a "selfie" age where we hear and see people doing for themselves what traditionally would have been done by someone else. Now more than ever, we hear about the importance of self-care. In reality, there is nothing wrong with taking care of ourselves. In fact, it's very important. The way to self-absorption is to not consider anyone else in anything that you do. I'm here to remind you of these words that have been spoken by so many: "Put God First in everything you do!"

One thing that I am consistent with is applying the thing that I am passionate about to every area of my life. In doing so, therein you'll find excellence in everything that I do, with the help of God. With that being said, as much as I thought about my position prior to the abortion and how the choices that I made would impact me, I also had to consider the impact on others. I thought about what I didn't want for myself and that led me to where I am today. Some may think of it as being selfish because I didn't want the uncertainty of having a fatherless child, or how I was going to finish school and take care of a child and my own needs. The list goes on and on. Nonetheless, I made the self-conscious decision to move forward with my life with a new outlook. With all sincerity, I desired to have a spirit-led life with no chains from my past holding me back.

Moving forward, with a still determined mind, I continued my studies in school and met the man of my dreams who desired nothing more than a pure relationship with God and a committed relationship with me. With my initial short-term resistance to his pursuit, we became the best of friends and intimate lovers who wed after two years of courtship. Although we were very young, we both knew that we wanted a forever relationship and understood that we were not defined by what others thought to have been a failure or mistake. We didn't talk about a lot of future plans at the time, but one thing that I remember discussing was the name that we would like for a son if we had one. Robert wasn't sold on having a Jr. He said that he wanted his son to have his own identity. He wanted to name his son Malach. I wasn't moved by that, so I came with the compromise of the name

Malachi Jordan. "Jordan" was pretty prominent at the time. In the pursuit of happiness, Rob and I were pleased to announce my pregnancy just months after we moved into our own apartment. I was the most elated simply because of the fact that I still held on to the belief that having a child was a thing of the past for me. Knowing that God found me worthy of carrying my husband's seed was truly an honor. I was not sure of his sentiments, but mine were full of gratefulness from start to finish. Even from the space of having a nearly effortless conception, I feel as though God favored me.

(As it is written in the Law of the Lord, every male that openeth the womb shall be called holy to the Lord;) Luke 2:23 (KJV)

If you've ever heard me speak, somewhere in my dialogue you'll always hear me say that God always confirms His word. He's such a relational spirit, to the point that commitment holds residence within the heart of Him and every believer. From the moment I knew that I was pregnant, I was reminded of the value of faithfulness. While it can be a scary thing to surrender to, it is also the most rewarding when endured through the challenges. I made the commitment to live my life according to what I believed was pleasing to God and from that moment, I've seen nothing but confirmations indicating that I was on the right track. During my time, people were on the fence as far as wanting to know the gender of the baby that they were expecting. As for us, we were the ones who did want to know, and sure enough, the ultrasound tech revealed that we were having a boy! Oh, what a feeling; my firstborn child; a male, the one we presented right back to God. Great is the faithfulness of God. Our son was born healthy and strong, witty and cute as a button!

Keeping in mind that Rob and I were still only 21 years old, married and now with a child, we were still striving to gain grounding for our lives. Every day was a faith walk and every moment we learned to trust each other and trust the path that we were on. We made strides and some we can say were misguided, but that commitment kept the torch lit to help us see our way through. The support of our parents was there, but I believe they allowed us to learn how to figure out our adult lives on our own. They provided insight, and we got straight forward direction, whether we liked it or not. All in all, we grew quickly from just the two of us to three, and then four, and then five.

Makayla and Destiny were my two loving angels that God had blessed us with, both just shy of being two years apart. Again, they were healthy, strong, witty, and beautiful. We managed to live our lives pretty decently. Our survival was predicated by our faith, hope, and trust in God. As a young wife and mother of three, I did what I could to support our family. With my husband being the breadwinner, I supported us by staying at home with our children and working home-based businesses and/or part-time evening jobs.

After living in a few rental properties and not appreciating the experience of living at the mercy of the owner's discretion, we were able to purchase our first home where I began operating my own daycare business, which was the best thing that had ever happened for our family on so many levels. I was able to fully meet the needs of my children, support our family income and help other families along the way.

I didn't mention much about the hardships and losses we faced in the time frame mentioned above for a reason. I wanted to recognize the goodness that we experienced during our young lives together. However, as we know, life comes with the good and the bad. Those unforeseen times did come during our presentation as the young Peterson couple. We began to experience death in our family beginning with my mother and literally within a two-year timeframe we lost another parent and even a sibling of Robert's. With the losses that we endured, we've also encountered the miracles of having two additional daughters added to our family tree.

Our young family had to learn how to lean and depend on each other with the examples laid before us to carry on as maturing adults and leaders of the family. This transformation was challenging, but because we knew we needed each other to survive, we maintained the life of loving and supporting each other no matter what. Surely there were disagreements leading individuals to go their own way as far as siblings were concerned, but we manage to keep connected to ensure that there was no love lost. Our children grew up knowing that God, love, and commitment are very important components of family life.

One major life transition outside of death that my family had watched me experience was the trauma from the attack on my childcare business, license, and career. After 15 years of service, for the first time ever, I was under an investigation that questioned my integrity, and that tried to defile my name. All of this happened when I was in the process of acquiring my dream of a fully operational daycare center outside of my home. As that dream was broken, my husband and children stood by and supported me along the way. I know that through this experience there was something that I had to learn, which includes letting go of the bitterness towards the people involved. I had to forgive them and outwardly speak my forgiveness towards them. After, I took time to really focus on my purpose in life. I took a deep dive into understanding myself and my experiences, and I sought God for complete direction for the furtherance of my life. I know my experiences were not only meant for me to get something out of them, but also to share and guide others in their journey of life. As I continue throughout the rest of my days, I will remain prayerful concerning my next steps. My gratefulness for my previous life lessons helps me to know that I am able to press reset and seek God for the direction and plan set forth. As human beings, everyone wants to fulfill their highest, truest expression of themselves, and I believe it is all possible through the hand of Him.

As a woman, I found my strength through spirituality, examples of other very important women in my life, as well as the village around me. As a mother, I followed the examples of the same. My mother and mother-in-law would say, "Eat the meat and spit out the bones." The phrase didn't do much for me at the time outside of having me think, "yuck." However, when I heard it the second time, it applied to my life, and I realized the value of absorbing the moments, time, and words shared with us as we journey along the way.

Wisdom comes in all shapes and sizes, forms, and presentations. It is up to us as individuals on how and when it is received. When you ask for wisdom, it is freely given. When you seek the right way, you will find it. What you are looking for is waiting for you to find it. The key to transformation is committing to the process.

"Blessed is everyone that feareth the Lord; that walketh in His ways. Forthou shalt eat the labour of thine hands: happy shalt thou be, and it shall be well with thee." Psalm 128:1-2

About *Tawana M. Peterson*

Tawana M. Peterson, a native of Hartford, CT, was born on November 24, 1975 to the late Richard L. Hill, Jr. and Bertha D. Holloman Hill. As an undergraduate at Johnson & Wales University, she met and shortly after became the wife of Robert L. Peterson and is now a proud mother of five amazing children. As a young wife and mother, Tawana pursued life as an entrepreneur to help support their family. In doing so, she became the owner of Smarty Pantz Early Education Center. Beginning in January 2020, Smarty Pantz Education and Resources (S.P.E.A.R.) launched it's consulting for aspiring Early Education Providers. In continued pursuit of supporting children and families, Tawana began to advocate for healthy, long-lasting marriages and is now one of the founders of The Marriage Grit, officially established on August 3, 2018. Although the launching of The Marriage Grit took place in recent years, the mission of supporting and mentoring couples has taken place since the conception of her marriage to Robert on August 3, 1996. Entrepreneurship is life for Tawana as is blood through the veins of her body. Her passion to keep these entities alive is her major priority. Tawana has been commissioned to be a light for human services and intends on fulfilling this call through everything that she puts her hands on.

Dear Diary:

"His lack of response should not dictate what type of day I should have!"

DISMANTLING OUR "HAPPY" HOME

T.C. Woodards

There is nothing in the world like a mother's love because it is a feeling that cannot be explained. Being a mother is the most rewarding job in the world and the most difficult because the responsibility does not come with an instruction manual.

I had to make the decision to dismantle our "happy" home because I was miserable and fed up with the infidelity that was going on behind my back. Prior to discovering that the individual that I was married to was living a double life, I contemplated leaving him several times. Every time I started saving secret money for my escape, something would come up and I had to use the money towards a bill or something for the kids. My initial plan was to save up enough money for a couple of years and then leave. Well, that did not happen the way that I anticipated.

It all started one week prior to Father's Day. I was faced with the reality that it was time to start removing myself from the toxic marriage because things went too far this time. I received the confirmation of what my gut was telling me the past year. My thorough investigation revealed that he had a side chick that he was spending time with every single chance that he could. The last straw for me was when I discovered that my kids were exposed to the affair because he thought that it was okay to bring our kids around her. I found out when I went through the text messages in his phone. His phone told the entire story about the double life he was living.

He was acting extremely weird one day, so I decided to run his phone and check his text messages because my woman intuition was telling me that something was not right. I waited until he fell asleep so I could install an app on his phone that emailed the entire text conversation to me. I uninstalled the app when I was finished and put the phone back where he left it. The kids were very sad, confused, and upset during this difficult time because they were young; my daughter was 10 years old, and my son was seven years old at the time all this chaos was going on. He violated our innocent kids by pulling them into his world of lies and deceit. I was devastated and felt so bad for my kids because they are innocent human beings that are supposed to be protected by their parents.

Not only did he cheat on me, he disrespected our kids by forcing them to watch their dad blatantly disrespect their mom. Even though I was pissed off about the fact that he had an affair, I was more hurt and pissed off about the fact that he exposed our kids to his secrets, lies, and affair. I was shocked and in disbelief that the individual that I was married to could do this horrible thing to our children. The more I thought about what happened to the kids, the angrier I became because I could not wrap my head around the fact that a person would even think that this kind of action was okay. It takes a "special" type of individual to do something like that to their kids. It was obvious that he did not take our kids' best interest into consideration because he confirmed that putting his needs first was more important than the family.

Every time that I looked at my kids, my heart broke into a million pieces over and over again because I could not imagine how they were feeling on the inside as they were witnessing their dad interacting with the side chick. I also became infuriated with myself for not leaving when I initially planned. Then again, who knows if that would have really been the case because it was obvious that he was very comfortable with taking them around her. I was concerned about how this experience was going to affect them mentally, emotionally, and psychologically. I knew that my decision to divorce their dad was going to impact them drastically because he was a part of their lives since birth.

I made the difficult decision to leave and find us another place to live because the home that we were living in was becoming more toxic and dysfunctional as the days dragged along. At the time, my kids were young and did not fully understand what was going on between their parents. I made it a priority to talk to them about the changes that were happening in our lives. The first thing that I did was start shopping for apartments during my lunch breaks. I did all the research and made the phone calls while I was at work because I did not want him to know that we were leaving until I secured us a new home. I made appointments to look at apartments during my lunch breaks, before work, after work, and on the weekends. I did not want my kids to be included in this process because they were already going through so much. When I found an apartment that I could afford by myself, I informed them that we were moving to our own house because mommy and daddy were not getting along and were always arguing.

At first, I felt guilty about leaving because I did not want my kids to think that I broke up the family. That feeling of guilt came from me witnessing their dad telling them that he had to leave the house because he made a mistake and mommy will not forgive him. When he told the kids that lie, they were devastated and pleaded with me to forgive him. They had no idea what was really going on between us for the past six months. Moving out and preparing for divorce was the best choice that I ever made because things would have gotten worse if I had stayed and continued to put up with the infidelity and abuse.

It was my duty as their mother, to protect them and keep them safe so removing them from a toxic home was the best decision for this terrible situation. The transition was very difficult for all three of us because the kids were mad at me for leaving and they took their anger out on me. They did not understand that the decision that I made was best for them because if I stayed, I would have been giving them the message that it is okay to be treated like that in a marriage and it is not. I did not want my son to think that it is okay to disrespect women, and

I did not want my daughter to think that it was okay to be disrespected. They were watching me, and it was my job as their mother to be a good role model.

After we settled into our new place of residence, I had a long heart-to-heart conversation with my kids and explained to them that unexpected things happen in life that we cannot control sometimes. I also explained to them that whatever happens between their parents that we both love them, and the situation is not their fault. The last thing that I stated was that no matter what they go through in life, never let the situation define who they are as a person. I encouraged them to continue excelling and doing what they need to do in school. I also decided to put us in family counseling so we could get through the separation process and prepare them for the divorce that was going to happen. The divorce process was extremely difficult for me and the kids because I had to stay strong for them while I was breaking on the inside. I felt so alone because the people closest to me had no idea what I was going through. The entire process was very messy because I was dealing with a spiteful individual who was bitter because I decided to walk away from our marriage. He told me on several occasions that I did not have to leave, I chose to leave. He really thought that I should have continued to tolerate his infidelity.

As I was waiting for my divorce to be finalized, I was in fear of my life because things turned really bad between us. He started stalking me and taunting me every day. I had to file several Emergency Protection from Abuse (PFA) Orders because he threatened to kill me several times. It got to the point that I had to let a few of my closest relatives know that if something happens to me, he did it! Despite all the drama, I received the best birthday gift: an approved divorce decree!

Making the decision to file for divorce was the best decision that I ever made because I am much happier without him and I enjoy my peace of mind to the fullest. Even though it was the toughest decision that I ever had to make, my kids are doing well and have adjusted to their parents being divorced. We have moved on with our new lives and are creating new memories. My mission was to create a loving and safe home environment that would help them to deal with what they had to go through. I made it my priority to tell my kids that sometimes things happen in life that we cannot control. I assured them that they were not the first kids whose parents divorced, and they would not be the last, and by the way they are adjusting, I think they understand that this was best for all of us.

About *T.C. Woodards*

T.C. Woodards is an inspiring divorced, single mom who has endured numerous life-changing experiences throughout her separation/divorce journey. She wrote and self-published her first book, *The Courage to Finally Walk Away* because she wanted to share her story to inspire and encourage individuals through similar life journeys. She is on a mission to enlighten, encourage, and empower women that are dealing with separation, divorce, co-parenting issues, and being a single parent. She uplifts and encourages individuals that are seeking support during their separation/divorce process. Individuals are comfortable with confiding in her because she has a genuine spirit and listens without judgment. Resiliency has led her to adapt well to trauma, tragedy, and significant sources of stress such as family/relationship problems, serious health problems, and financial hardships. She is also the owner of TCW Publishing LLC.

Dear Diary:

"Lord, you are simply amazing. I can see how you are preparing me and why you have given me some of the instructions you have."

DRIVING THE PICKLE BUS ON A GUILT TRIP
Ursula McCoy

"Just dropped the boy off… on my way to get the girl..."
"Headed to Jersey for the boy's tournament..."
"In New York for the girl's competition..."
"Gotta pick the girl up at 9 p.m., but headed to pick the boy up first because he finishes at 8 p.m."

Well, that's "where we are" so let's go back to "where it started." This Pickle Bus fired up its engine around 2011-ish. But first, the backstory...

Around 2009, approaching the age of 32, I was a single mother doing everything in my power to make ends meet. As an educator, early in my career, I capitalized on every opportunity to earn extra money, therefore, I coached three sports, served as a class advisor, stayed after school for this, came in early for that, and anything else there was to earn a few extra dollars in my paycheck. They (whoever 'they' are) say, with money comes sacrifice and this couldn't be any more accurate. Although I was earning extra money to care for me and my son, otherwise affectionately known as "The Boy Child", the sacrifice came in my time spent with him. It was only me and him living in a small two-bedroom apartment in New Castle, Delaware at the time, and the only time we were there was to sleep. I spent all my time at work while he spent all his time at school and then aftercare, which, in my eyes, worked well for me. It allowed me to work long hours and pick him up when I was finished. Most days, he was the first one there and the last one to leave. Eventually, I was able to afford to send him to one of the best private schools in the state–a private school that he admired for the sports it offered and begged to attend after watching them compete in the state championship. Even at the age of 6, he had "hoop dreams" of surrounding himself with the best.

Here I was, in my early 30s, and I found myself overworked, underpaid. As much as I loved what I was doing for my students and my school community, I was stressed and depressed. Stressed from caring for my own aging parents, raising a son by myself, working on my master's degree and giving all of my energy to my students and my athletes. Depressed in that many nights were sleepless, and many mornings greeted me with a tear-soaked pillow. I knew I had to take control over my life once I lost over an inch of hair from the back of my neckline up. As much as I attempted to embed myself into the Word of God, there was still something missing, like some sort of physical activity to take my mind off my life. I was an athlete, and the answer was simple; so, to relieve my stress and erase my depression, I returned to the sport I loved most: volleyball. Volleyball was always "it" for me. It kept me grounded, released the frustration, and I felt centered, balanced as I navigated through life's journey. Therefore, I joined an adult league to play weekly. We played on Wednesday nights and sometimes our games started as late as 9 p.m. I dragged my son out of the apartment to sit in the bleachers as I attempted to center myself in a world of chaos, a world that left me drained day in and day out. A world that didn't seem to care if I fell apart; a world that would lend me a hand, but only to use that same hand to push me deeper into my secret world of darkness.

I recall the song "Smile" by recording artist Tamia being the theme-song of my life.

> *'Cause you never let 'em see you sweat*
> *Don't want them to think the pain runs deep*
> *Lord knows it's killing me*

And so I put on my make up
Put a smile on my face
And if anyone asks me
Everything is okay
I'm laughing 'cause no one
Knows the joke is on me
But I'm dying inside
With my pride and a smile
On my face
It's not an easy thing to do
Sometimes it's hard to face the truth
It's not the life that I would choose
But what else can I do?

But what else can I do? I felt that this is not the life I was supposed to live. I felt that my decisions and choices for my life landed me in a place where my back was against the wall to provide for my son, to put him into positions in life so that he wouldn't become a statistic as I felt I had become. I almost felt like I was torturing myself in an attempt to regain a sense of power and control of my life.

Fast forward a few years, around 2011, my master's degree was complete, my father passed, and I was transferred to a new school for work, which meant I was no longer coaching or fulfilling other job responsibilities. The only thing that was still true to my life was The Boy Child and volleyball. As much as my son and I loved one another, and as much fun as we were having with this newfound time I had, there was still a sadness that existed; something was missing in his life. I knew my father's death took a toll on him. His older brother moved away, and his male cousin moved as well. I attributed his sadness to the fact that he was having issues adjusting to all the male-figures in his life disappearing one-by-one. I searched for mentoring groups, but unfortunately, there weren't many around for a not-so-troubled five-year-old dealing with an adjustment disorder.

One Wednesday night, I looked over in the corner of the gym and saw the boy child peacefully dribbling a volleyball non-stop and it clicked! I found my answer! I found my balance in sports, so why didn't I realize sooner that maybe he would too? The same night, I went home and researched youth basketball leagues. I found i9 Sports, CIA, and YMCA. By the next day, I registered him for all three! From that moment, the Pickle Bus was on the road!

The Pickle Bus stems from the Sweet Pickles series of children's books written by Perle, Reinach, and Hefter in the 1970s. The books tell the stories of animal-based characters that find themselves in a "Pickle" or a difficult situation because of their human-like personalities. The set of books came with activities that were housed in a plastic container shaped like a bus. I soon transformed my car into the pickle bus, full of stories and activities based on my Sweet Pickle and his adventures. The difficult situation in all of this, you ask? Well, trying to balance his schedule of school, multiple leagues, with mine of work, playing volleyball, advancing my career, and caring for an elderly parent who was mourning and grieving the loss of her husband of over 45 years was no easy task. Not to mention I enrolled him in piano and drum lessons, mime at church, and karate on top of basketball, but I was determined to let my son know this was his time to shine and that he would no longer play the background of my ripping and running. If I was going to be all over the place, it would be because he was living out his dreams.

Years went by and I was still driving the Pickle Bus to and from, tournament after tournament, camp after camp, practice after practice. I was dedicated and determined to drive this bus until the wheels fell off. Then low and behold, in 2014, the Pickle Bus would double in size. The Girl Child was born. Although some thought that would slow us down, it didn't. Her father worked a very busy schedule, sometimes almost 20 hours a day with little to no sleep in between jobs. As much as I would have loved to leave her home and away from the hectic life the Boy Child and I had signed up for, it just didn't happen. Therefore, we packed her diaper bag, buckled her up into her car seat and kept the bus rolling. There were days I prayed, hoping she would not get lost in her brother's shadow and become his personal traveling cheerleader. As a woman who grew up in sports, played in high school, and received multiple athletic scholarships in college, I didn't want my precious princess to lose the opportunity to realize her talent and pursue any dreams she may have just like her brother.

Very early in my pregnancy, I realized she was strong and mighty; it was shortly after her birth that I experienced her desire to climb. The more I attempted to cradle and cuddle with her, the more she attempted to break free and climb up my shoulder and into the air. She loved being whirled around and flipped upside down. I knew then gymnastics would be the sport I'd start her in as soon as she was old enough to go. Reaching out to my best friend, whose daughter was and is a rising gymnastics star for suggestions, I found a gym that would take her as early as 18-months. I circled the date on a calendar and could not wait. She was walking, or should I say running by nine months, and climbing on any and everything she could find by the time she turned one. She loved bouncy houses and playgrounds, so 18 months couldn't come soon enough. I had to give this bubbly personality something to channel her energy.

I couldn't love these two anymore! They were amazing; however, I was in the midst of a personal breakdown. Behind the scenes of my life, I was falling apart. Nothing was progressing the way I planned, which became a constant reminder that my life is according to God's plan, not mine. Back in school to elevate my career once again, I often found myself on my 45-minute drive to class in a quiet fog. No radio, no phone, just me and my thoughts. One night, my professor pulled me to the side and had a long "mother-daughter" talk with me. It was exactly what I needed to stop looking through the rearview mirror and start looking through the front windshield of my life. The rearview mirror is smaller for a reason. It's there only to give you a glimpse of your past and where you have traveled from. The windshield is ahead of you and is where your focus should be as you move ahead. My perspective changed and so did my journey.

The summer of 2015 was approaching, the boy was wrapping up his AAU season, and the girl was about 17 months old, just shy of the 18-month-old requirement to sign up for the summer session of the Mommy & Me gymnastics class. I called and pleaded my case, as I knew there was no way I could wait any longer to get this girl into something to burn all the energy she had. They graciously agreed to let her join the class, and it forever changed her life. Her teacher was phenomenal! She loved it and I loved her loving it! It was perfect for her; she could climb, hang, run, bounce, and jump off things. She was truly in her element.

The summer went on, the boy in basketball camp after basketball camp and the girl at Mommy & Me classes every Saturday. Week in and week out, we followed the same routine until the summer ended and it was time to start school again. Daily basketball camp turned into basketball practice once or twice a week in the evenings and then tournaments on the weekends. We never knew in advance when the weekend games would be, so it was difficult to continue the Saturday gymnastics classes. I always felt that since I was the one who signed the Pickles up for their activities, it was my responsibility to make sure they attended. Asking for help has always been my biggest weakness. I never wanted a decision I made for them to be a burden on someone else, and because of this, I did not continue the girl's gymnastics classes.

Winter came and went, and so did spring. With each passing season, I felt I was neglecting my daughter, and she was becoming the one thing I did not want her to become, her Bro Bro's personal traveling cheerleader. When summer arrived, I signed her up for classes again and was determined to keep her in them throughout the year. When it was time for the fall session to start, I found out the teacher we loved would not be her teacher if we continued to the next level of classes and based on reviews, I went hunting for a new gym for her to receive a quality experience. I went to the best resource I knew who would be 100% honest, my best friend. She told me where her daughter was training and the growth she had seen since going there. So, we went with it. The only thing was, this gym was in the neighboring state of Pennsylvania and by this time, the boy was also playing basketball in another neighboring state, New Jersey. Then the self-debates started, and the guilt trip began. Did I really want to start this travel life for my then three-to-four-year-old? Was that a bit extreme? I was already traveling 40-plus miles one way to take the boy to practice a few nights a week. Did I really want to add taking the girl across state lines for a Mommy & Me gymnastics class? I mean, it's not like I was trying to create an Olympic gymnast. From this, more of the guilt trip set in. If I could drive my son all the way into South Jersey multiple times a week, surely, I could drive 10 miles to take my daughter to burn some energy once a week. So, I did.

After a few months of realizing that I had bitten off far more than I could chew, I decided not to continue with the girl's classes in Pennsylvania, saying I would revisit the idea when it made more sense. Again, it's not like she was going to the Olympics and my son currently had aspirations of playing at a higher level, so the greater investment had to be him, or so I thought. With an AAU national championship, middle school tournament championships, and soon to be conference championships under his belt, plus training from some of the best basketball minds in the area, the boy was well underway to accomplishing his dreams of playing at higher levels. The girl was approaching five years old and had yet to become consistent in the very thing that was the most natural for her. She was still quite the bouncing bean and climber. By now she had made a habit of finding her way to the top shelf of anything that had a top shelf, being upside down at any chance given, and jumping across my furniture like a Wipe Out obstacle course.

God, being as awesome as He is, heard my prayers and one day my best friend told me of a new local Black-owned gym I should check out. This was perfect! It was close, it was affordable, and it was owned by a Black former gymnast, that I knew of and whose two daughters were both in the sport. We signed up for classes and my baby girl loved every minute of it. Session after session for a full year, I was able to give my daughter the outlet she needed to foster the skills and the energy she exerted. Nearing the end of the spring session of classes, the owner handed me an envelope with a letter inside. This letter was an invitation for my girl to join the competition team. *THE COMPETITION TEAM?! Wait a minute!* I thought to myself. *She has fun at gymnastics, but is she good enough for the competition team? I've seen her cartwheel!* The only thing she has really accomplished was being upside down, which is one of her favorite past times. Yes, she may have been strong, but I surely didn't think the competition team would be for her. There was nothing graceful about her. She was like a bull in a china shop. So, after a lot of second guessing and double checking with the owners, they assured me she had the potential and the talent for what it takes to be a competitive gymnast. I guess that's why they are the professionals; this is what they get paid to do, right?

So, the investment begins—time and money—as gymnastics takes a lot of both. She went from one hour of classes a week to eight hours of practice per week, and the Pickle Bus picked up on mileage. I found myself dropping one off, then the other, then turning around to pick the first one up, and then eventually backtracking to pick up the other. Dinner came from a drive thru on most nights on our way to New Jersey or on our way home from New Jersey and they usually completed homework under the interior light of my car. Rarely were we ever home before 9 p.m. after leaving in the morning at 6 a.m. My mother was concerned we were doing too much, which looking back at it, I am sure we were. I am sure this was not healthy for a five and twelve/thirteen-year-old, but they were in their element and I refused to stop for the sake of being home to rest or relax. Instead, we hopped on the Pickle Bus and made life happen.

The more and more they grew and advanced in their sports, the more and more I became drained. My 40th birthday came, and my theme was supposed to be "40 & Fantabulous". Instead, it turned into "40 & Fell Apart." Blood clots, blood thinners, tests, iron infusions, surgeries & procedures all took over my life. I did everything in my power to keep up The Pickles and their schedules, but I was exhausted, and I was tired. The more I tried to help myself, the less it actually helped, but I refused to let my babies down. I was their number one supporter, so come hell or high water, I had to make it happen, no matter the toll it took on me.

By the summer of 2019, the boy added more championships to his resume, and the girl spent seven months training before her first competition. I was used to watching him compete, but I was nervous for her. *What if she messes up? How will she take it? Will she cry and want to give up? Did I put her into something that she wasn't ready for? Will she freeze up?* OMG! I wasn't ready! Just a few months ago, she fell apart when it was time for an exhibition performance at the local minor-league baseball game. Would she do the same in front of the judges? The time had come for The Gingerbread Invitational in Salisbury, MD, and there was no turning back. Her father, brother, and I got shirts made to show we were there to support her, we drove south to Maryland, and we had our cameras ready to document this monumental moment. We watched her warm-up, and she looked amazing! She seemed confident, poised, and excited. She was in the hands of her coaches and there was nothing I could do to save or protect my baby girl, who although tough like her mommy, was still my baby.

The competition began, and she crushed it! She came home with three first place medals and one second place. She also finished first all-around! I couldn't believe it; my baby was a natural. She was literally born for this. Meet after meet, we traveled up and down the East Coast from Maryland to New York and it was the same thing; the girl child was in her element, shining bright like a star, and I couldn't be happier. Meanwhile, the boy was continuing to win games and subsequently, the second of a back-to-back Catholic League Championship. He was preparing for what was to be a very pivotal AAU season, as he was also deciding what high school to attend. Everything in life was important, everything was a major decision.

Then Covid-19 happened. The virus shut everything down for my Pickles and The Pickle Bus was parked. The Boy Child became severely depressed and angry, while The Girl Child became antsy as all get out. Cabin fever set in and there was nothing I could do to help besides move my car from the driveway so the boy could shoot around and continue to order as much gymnastics equipment from Amazon as my house could hold for the girl to flip around. I had to dig down deep into my mom-mind to find ways to fix this for them, only to realize I did not know how to navigate my children through this unprecedented time. I felt swamped with my own workload of trying to operate a school remotely, stay on them about their schoolwork and classes, and get them to understand what was happening in the world around us. I tried to give them compassion, grace, and space to have the emotions they had during this time of confusion. The girl seemed to handle it far better than the boy who simultaneously reached the peak of adolescence during a national quarantine. I asked God, "What prayer did I have that this was the test or the answer?"

As I reflect, mom-guilt has been a driving factor in many of the decisions I have made over the years. Whether I felt guilty that I was not available to my children due to work, so I cut some of my responsibilities out, guilty that I picked them up while talking on the phone to friends, so I ignored the calls so I could talk to my children in the car, guilty that I wasn't making enough money to provide a two-income household, so I went back to school to elevate my career, or even guilty that they would be raised by a single mother, so I stayed in relationships longer than I should have. Guilt trip after guilt trip, I did what I felt was needed to provide a better life for my children. But Covid-19 wasn't "guilt," there was nothing I could do to fix the pandemic, and that, in and of itself, made me feel terrible and made me feel guilty. My children could not do the very things that became their passion, their motivation, their reason why.

It wasn't until having my back against the wall that I completely understood that I am not in control over every aspect of my life and definitely not every aspect of my children's lives. It was then that I redefined my role in their life as their *support* system and no longer their *control* system. I accepted that I do not have all the answers and that I cannot fix everything that goes wrong in their lives, but most importantly, that it was ok for this to be the case. I trust in God in all that I do, so I had to trust that where I fell short, He would be there to pick up the pieces.

God knows my children are my weakness and for them I will sacrifice all that I have and everything within me. I have proven to Him that these blessings bestowed upon me in human form are my top priority on Earth, and for them, I will go without. For them, I have gone without. I understood that God has equipped me with everything that I need to provide a solid foundation for my children to grow upon and that teaching them to advocate for themselves in addition to becoming productive members of society is enough.

Perfection is not attainable, and the Lord knows I have my share of flaws. I continue to struggle with the guilt associated with being a single mother. I often find myself in a quiet room questioning where I went wrong and if my mistakes are beyond repair. There are days I think I have given too much of myself to my children, mostly the Boy Child, because I don't feel that at 14 years old, he appreciates all that I have done and all that I have sacrificed for him, but as long as my heart is true to God and to them, I have to remind myself I am doing all I can do. Even when the doubt kicks in, even when the times are the toughest, and most of all, even when tears fall to the point where there are no tears left, I have to remind myself that I am doing everything that I know how to do and everything within my power to support him and his sister throughout their life's journey.

The moment I spoke life over our lives and spoke affirmations over my struggles is the moment things turned around. The proverbial light at the end of the tunnel appeared and simultaneously, the state started to open, sports were reinstated, and the Pickle Bus was revved up and ready to get back on the road. It started slowly with a practice here, training there, workout classes on Zoom, but now the boy is playing high school basketball where he accomplished one of his goals of playing varsity as a freshman; the girl is competing as a level two gymnast, placing in the top three in just about every event at every competition, setting records for her gym, and is currently training 22.5

hours a week to potentially become an elite gymnast and possibly skip competition levels next season. As for me, I have learned that it is ok to have a tear in my Supermom cape and that although I still struggle with it, it is okay to reach out and ask for help. Let me repeat that... *I still struggle, and it is ok.* Grace and space are the two allowances I have afforded myself to get through the ongoing rollercoaster of my life. Currently, most days, when I receive a phone call, somewhere in the conversation, usually right after, "Hey Urs, what are you up to?", my response is something along the lines of:

"Just dropped the boy off, on my way to get the girl,"
"Headed to Jersey for the boy's tournament,"
"In New York for the girl's competition," or
"Gotta pick the girl up at 9 p.m., so I'm headed to pick the boy up first because he finishes at 8 p.m."

And I wouldn't have it any other way.

About *Ursula McCoy*

Born on December 5, 1977 and raised in Newark, Delaware, Ursula McCoy is one of two children born to William, Sr. and Annette Cornish. Along with her older brother William, Jr., he and Ursula were both educated in the Christina School District. An early walker at 6 months, Ursula was very active from the beginning. She began her athletic talents in gymnastics, ballet, tap, and jazz styles of dancing in which she continued for approximately 10 years. Then she was introduced to the sport of volleyball in which she found her passion. Volleyball opened many doors for Ursula as she played in high school and received a full scholarship at South Carolina State University. There, she excelled as an All-MEAC conference player and received a host of awards and accolades for the school. It's no wonder both of her children, Elin Jahmeere (15) and Justyce Roi (7) are rising athletic stars in their own rights. Currently, Ursula is a school administrator serving as an Assistant Principal in the Colonial School District. Having been in education for over 20 years, Ursula devotes herself and her time to helping her students develop their full potential as scholars and athletes. She is driven by the words spoken in Jeremiah 29:11, *"For I know the plans I have for you, declares the Lord, plans to prosper you, and not to harm you, plans to give you hope and a future."* It is through these words that Ursula attempts to inspire all with whom she comes in contact with.

Dear Diary:

"Making note of Gods faithfulness."

A MOTHER'S WORST NIGHTMARE
Virginia A. Clark

Have you ever felt like you've eaten something that just got stuck in the throat and you've tried everything… hot tea, water, etc. but you just could not swallow it? That's what my life has been for the past five years.

April 2, 2015

It was a beautiful, slightly brisk April morning. I woke about 6:30 to take my morning walk–just a normal day, but as I walked, I saw the geese flying above and they were in a V formation. I started thinking how amazing it is that there's always a lesson in the still of the morning. As the geese flew above, I noticed there was one that fell out of the formation. When this happens, there's always that shepherd goose that goes back to get the fallen goose and puts it back in formation, and then they carry on.

This reminds me of two scriptures, one from I Peter 2:25 (ESV), which reads: *"For you were like sheep going astray,"* but now you have returned to the Shepherd and Overseer of your souls" and the other from Ezekiel 34:15 (ESV): *"I myself will be the shepherd of my sheep, and I myself will make them lie down, declares the Lord God."*

What a great lesson in the still of the morning! As I walked back home, I marveled at the lessons that I've learned as I walk and talk with Jesus. I got home, got dressed, and headed to work about 9 a.m. and I had a very productive day. By 5 p.m., I headed home, excited to spend time with my son and husband, who at the time was driving trucks overnight, and FaceTime my youngest daughter, who was attending college in Boston.

That Dreadful April morning

April 3, 2015 was the beginning of the longest ordeal as a mother that I could even contemplate going through. A true nightmare, just a true nightmare. It was Good Friday morning. The house was quiet. My son had just walked his pregnant fiancé to the door. My husband and I were in bed after a long day of work. Around 4 a.m., our then 1-year-old Yorkshire terrier got very agitated, and he insisted on going outside.

Much to our surprise, it was because the house was surrounded by police. My husband got up and let him out the back door, still very groggy from being in a deep sleep. As he opened the back door, cops were breaking down the front door with a battering ram. I will never forget that horrific sound; it sounded like an A-bomb. They all came charging in, rushing up the stairs. All I remember hearing is "Wilmington Police!" and orders from detective telling police where to go.

The next thing I knew, there was a 6-foot-tall police officer standing over my head with his weapon drawn as I laid there, and then a second police officer followed his lead. The police officer standing over me shouted, "Put your hands up!"

I remember shouting, "Get out of my room!" The police officer allowed me to get up and grab my robe and then he escorted me downstairs. As I navigated down the stairs, I wanted to know where my husband was. I could see that they had my son's hands tied sitting on the couch in my living room. I was very concerned for my husband because they startled him, and he didn't get a lot of rest since he is a truck driver. He was a bit shaken up and was outside trying to catch his breath.

That moment was very devastating. I felt as though my house had been invaded for no reason. When I asked for a warrant, they gave me a piece of paper, and as I tried to read it, one police officer said, "You can read that later." Then I asked where the county police was because we live in the county. I was told that the county police officer had been there, but he left.

As the morning progressed, they searched portions of our house and stated they were looking for a weapon for a crime that happened over a year prior. The reason for intruding on our home was still a mystery because my son was on probation, which he had checked in prior to that week! I didn't understand why the big element of surprise was necessary.

As the officers carried my son handcuffed out of our home, my son asked, "Can I give my mother a kiss?" and the officer said, "Yes, kiss your mom now, because you will never see her again."

Can you imagine if a building had feelings before the day and time that it was scheduled to explode? What would that feeling be like? What would the emotions be? Well, let me humanize it for you. It's an out-of-body experience of whys, this can't be, what can I do to stop this madness, who can I reach out to right now... Lord make them stop!

Too late. It's done.

My son wrote a poem from his point of view and I want to include it here because I am him, and he is me. My son's poem is parallel to how I was feeling.

The Warrant
Intuition wake me up now I'm walking to the stairs
And I see flashlights shining everywhere
I hear loud shouts (police, police!)
This is a nightmare, but no, I ain't sleep
I hear so many voices, damn they sound Deep
I hear a loud boom then I hear their shoes squeak
I got nowhere to run, Fear make me lay down
Plus, I ain't trying to get shot right now
Now they're in my room, guns pointed to my head
I know if I make the wrong move, then I'm dead
They asked me my name, but my Rights ain't get read

147

Yeah, that's him, that's what the one cop said
I look the one in the eyes that cuff me with the zip ties
He got on a mask, but I think I know the guy
Two of them pick me up raise me to my feet
I hear someone mention gun it rhyme if I say heat
That's what they looking for, this room bout to get sweep'd
this ain't regular police man this is safe street
Looney and his crew I'm like wat the fuck I do?
Plus, they dirty as fuck, they'll plant shit on you.
Walking down these stairs
I'm greeted by these awkward stares.
At the moment, I don't see my parents anywhere.
What they looking for, I don't got, so I don't care.
I'm jus glad that my pregnant wifey wasn't there
A room full of smiles on every body's face
But someone to my right just looks outta place
A vest... no gun... she staying out the way
I'm assuming that must be the DA
Now I see my parents, I hear this black cop say
I know that he mad he getting locked up today
Two cops lying to my parents saying everything gone b ok
a bald head white dude a chick that look like jean gray
Not the one from the cartoons the one from the movies
Man, these niggas happier than some motha fuckin
    groupies
All this for a gun that I don't got, man I'm thinking that
    I'm cool
but my gut saying this a Lil too much for a tool
They tryna start a fire but who gave them the fuel
breaking laws and lying that ain't playing by the rules what
    I do... shit
I guess it ain't important I still haven't seen a Affidavit or
    a warrant

But why instead of asking questions I just sit back and sigh
   sitting across from my dad and mom watching tears
   form in her eye.
It's breaking my heart watching my mom cry.
I can't help but think that this all started from a lie!

Have you ever opened your eyes in the still of the morning and looked to the heavens and said, "Lord, let it be the day after today because I can't bear to go through this day"?

This was the feeling of the first day my child had to face trial proceedings. Imagine sitting in a court room, staring at strangers. You're praying they can read your heart without you uttering a word, praying they are not looking at you as just another brown face with freedom of expression all over you in the form of tattoos, judging you from how you look on the outside versus the inward spirit of the man.

The only thing I thought was "Lord, I wish I could take this pain away for my child!" all the while struggling to breathe.

Watching my child from the jail cell window

Elephants are my favorite creature, but just imagine you as a real human and an elephant steps on your chest—you're not able to breathe. That's the feeling of riding by the prison knowing that your child is in this God-forsaken place, not knowing what he is going through at that very moment, the pain of the weight of the elephant on your chest is unbearable, but I digress.

Through conversations with my son and his private investigators, I learned that the driver in the case had been questioned but not detained or charged behind his involvement. I was truly puzzled. I was being told the driver gave a different account than the codefendant—an account where my son is now the driver. This clearly contradicts what the codefendant had agreed to testify to an open court on a recording. So, the driver was clearly being coerced.

The codefendant told a version of the story where there are five people in the car. He places my son as one gun man, another man as a gun man, a driver and two innocent bystanders, one being himself. He tells the story of how they pull over on the side of a road, that my son and another man exit the car, walk up a street, fire, and kill a man. He told this story on December 11, 2015 to prosecutors and homicide detectives hoping to obtain immunity from the crime. He mentioned the driver and another innocent bystander that could validate his story if what he was saying was the truth.

Speaking with my son, I reminded him of the book of Deuteronomy16:15-21where it reads:

(ESV): "A single witness shall not suffice against a person for any crime or for any wrong in connection with any offense that he has committed. Only on the evidence of two witnesses or of three witnesses shall a charge be established. If a malicious witness arises to accuse a person of wrongdoing, then both parties to the dispute shall appear before the Lord before the priests and the judges who are in office in those days. The judges shall inquire diligently, and if the witness is a false witness and has accused his brother falsely, then you shall do to him as he had meant to do to his brother. So, you shall purge the evil from your midst. ..."

The Warrant, Part 2

What kase u kno the getaway driver wasn't arrested
the validity to the driver's identity can't be contested
a co-d regurgitated what should have been digested
One of my co-defendants turned states witness is what I'm
    saying In essence
Going through the motions, the truth is something they
    never wanted to search
(Is)[why] they didn't wanna shed light where it couldn't b
    reversed
They said we can charge u will let u go repeat us like a verse
That's the personification of Someone bein coerced
But pay attention the co-d said the driver was driving
The police and the DA told the driver say I was driving
Can you decipher between who's telling the truth and
    who's lying

I kno this ain't making sense that's because it's something
they hiding.

The Trial

These are my journal entries during the trial.

September 5, 2017

Courtroom 8B

Got an urgent call at 7:15 from my son's attorney asking us to bring
clothes for his jury selection that was scheduled for the next day. The
attorney stated we needed to be there by 8:30 a.m. We are 30 to 40
minutes away with heavy traffic. Thank God we didn't unpack the
suitcases from a year ago when we were told a trial would start.

Later in the afternoon we got another call from the attorney
around 1:45 wanting to know if my husband and I were going to be at
the courthouse today, because trial was starting. It was supposed to
just be the jury selection *only*, or so we were told. I raced to the
courthouse alone because my husband had to work. Once I arrived, I
entered the courtroom and was told that I could not be in the court
room because I am on the list to testify for the state. Now I'm really
confused. Never was I sequestered by the state, but the bailiff escorted
me out of the court room. Yet another ploy to keep my son down!

Headed back home, confused, upset, not understanding what
game is being played. This is all a vicious circle, a roller coaster that I
don't even want to ride but was forced to ride anyway. The laws of the
land in the hands of corrupt authority will never be for you. You must
stay prayed up! You must stay woke, people! Most of all, you must trust
in God's plan and not man.

September 6, 2017

Courtroom 8B

We arrive at the courthouse at 9:10 a.m. with my mom, sister,
niece, best friend and her sister. My son's girlfriend is already in the
court room. As I sit outside wondering what lies are being told today
about my son, I am both mad and confused that I am still not allowed

in the court room because the state has decided that they might call me to the stand as a witness. I sat and prayed for the Lord to come down and to prick the hearts of these inhumane people. They lie just to lie, to save themselves, not thinking or caring about the lives that have been and will be changed forever.

I pray in Jesus' name. Begging you Father, to come down, remove all this pain from my family today and to allow the jury to see through all the lies and corruption. Amen.

September 7, 2017
Courtroom 8B

We arrive at 9:00 a.m. with my mom, sister, niece, my best friend and her sisters. Awaiting another day of lies and uncertainty of my son's life. As I sat and recapped what I was told of things that happened in the courtroom yesterday, I am still amazed at how all of this is allowed to play out in 2017, a time of great technology, like street cameras, etc. The constant lies are so very hurtful, and it is really scary that at any time a person's life can be removed due to untruths. The proceedings today should only last until 1:00 p.m., the state will rest, and Friday the prosecutor will start with his witnesses. I pray dear Lord please give my son strength today to get through all he needs to hear and help him to continue focusing on walking through the valley.

As I sit outside the courtroom and wait, so many different emotions run through my head, I want to just cry out. I'm scared, hurt, angry, nervous, hopeful but mostly prayerful.

Dear Lord, as we head home for the evening, please allow us all to rest peacefully, returning again tomorrow to press on in the lion's den. In your sweet name Jesus, I pray, Amen!

September 8, 2017
Courtroom 8C

We arrive at the courthouse at 11:30 a.m. with my mom, sister, niece, best friend, her sisters, and my minister. Still not allowed to enter the courtroom. As I walk to sit on the cold benches in the foyer one more day, I see the two investigators along with the prosecutor and a tall black male. The prosecutor walks out to advise the investigators that they are next to testify. I overhear the investigators ask the tall black male if he was ok now that the family of the victim has left the courtroom for a minute to catch their breath. I see that the male is a part of the victim's family.

Lord, my feelings today are all over the place. I pray this poor family realizes that my son is not a part of this ridiculous, sinful crime. Lord, please continue to move and rain down on this court, to see and have the truth revealed. I pray Lord that the young man who did this crime is taken care of by you Lord, and not the streets. Lord, I pray that you reveal all the others that have been hurt by this person in Jesus' name, Amen.

As I sat and waited for my family to come out and advise as to how the trial was going, a young man walked up to me, and he said, "I've noticed that you have been here for days." I replied, "Yes unfortunately, I have, and I will be here for another week."

He said, "I understand." He went on to explain that all will work out, because not that long ago, he was walking in the back of that same courtroom in shackles, and now he's walking through the front door of the courtroom as an attorney. To God be the glory!

September 11, 2017
Courtroom 8C

We arrive at the courthouse at 9:00 a.m. Still not allowed to enter the courtroom. My mom, sister, best friend, her two sisters, and my niece are all ready for the next proceedings to start. The judge would not allow my son's cellmate to enter the court to testify on his behalf, stating it would be repeating hearsay. The problem with this is that they allowed the state to use the testimony of an inmate from down south that's a member of the deceased's family. He was serving 33 years, hoping to turn states evidence in order to be released. The case today is all over the place. I had brief conversations with the private investigators, and they stated that the defense was not able to produce any of the witnesses that he had lined up. Now think about that, in a normal case, each side is supposed to know who the witnesses are going to be. Once again, corruption. Today, the state will cross-examine a known drug dealer and the young man that was identified as the murderer, but he turned state's evidence. As I sit and wait, I get word that my son's attorney wants to put him on the stand to testify. In most cases like this, that is known as suicide. I am very confused and very upset still. I am not able to enter the courtroom as a law-abiding citizen, and it is my rights to be able to enter.

My prayer today is dear Lord, as I sit and wait, Lord, I asked that you be with my son, the attorney and all involved, as they continue to search for the truth and justice. Lord, I beg of you to come down during these proceedings and show who You are to this very corrupt system here in Delaware. Lord, I continue to pray for the family of the deceased, for the mom, the children that have to endure this pain and suffering all over again from a man that took their loved one's life for no reason. I asked this in your name Jesus, Amen.

September 12, 2017
Courtroom 8B

We arrive at court today at 10:44 AM. Court was delayed due to the judge having things to take care of. My mom, sister, niece and my husband are in the courtroom today prayed up and ready for the Lord to control the situation.

I sit yet another day outside of the courtroom, awaiting the moment I can enter with great anticipation, but no doubt God will prevail today as he does every day. My prayer today is for the family of the deceased. I pray that God will continue to wrap his loving arms of comfort around them, for this has to be the most unsettling ordeal for them as a family to go through. I'm sure that day is replayed constantly in their minds, a simple family gathering turns tragic at the hands of a heartless individual. Lord, I pray for a stillness in their lives. I pray that they stay a strong family and continue to love their loved ones as well. Lord, I pray for all the lives in this case. Lord, I pray that you will continue to watch over the young men who are responsible for killing this man. I pray Lord that you prick their hearts and help them to see the wrong, and free themselves from sin, by telling the truth. I pray Lord, that they show remorse someday. I pray for the state prosecutor and judge who also knows the truth and refuses to abide by it. Lord, work on their hearts. You Lord have given them these positions to rule over the land. Lord, please go with the P.I.'s and the police of our community. The corruption is unreal. I ask for attention in this area, not asking to overlook any wrongdoing of the people, but for them to simply do the job that you have awarded them the opportunity to do. In Jesus' name, Amen.

September 13, 2017
Courtroom 8C

We arrive at the courthouse at 9:00 a.m. I am finally allowed to enter the courtroom. This is the day my son testifies on his own behalf and his attorney does the closing remarks. What a range of emotions I'm feeling right now. It is personal suicide to testify when the prosecutor is just going to rip him apart, put words in his mouth, twist what he is saying. The intense pressure is unbearable, but we believe in telling the truth, and as the Word says, "The truth shall set you free." I pray Lord, please go with my son as he reflects on the truth, that you give him the strength to speak, hold his head high, and clear up all the lies that have been told during this trial. Lord, I pray you prick the hearts of this jury, clear their minds and their souls, so that they hear his heart. In Jesus' name, Amen.

September 14, 2017
Courtroom 8C

Today is jury deliberation day. I arrive at my best friend's sister's house alone, as my family had to head back out of state, and husband headed to work out of town. My friend's sister lives only five minutes from the courthouse, so we planned to meet there to wait for the call from the attorney. Now we wait and pray. Around 1:00 p.m., we get a call that the jury is in and we head to the courthouse just to find out that the jury had a question to ask the judge. He answers the question and dismisses us until the next day.

September 15, 2017
Courtroom 8C

It's a solemn morning. as I head to my best friend's sister's house to wait to hear from the courts, I'm reminded of the day that I gave birth to my beautiful son. It was the 5th month and the 15th day. My life changed the day this little guy, my baby boy, my pride, was born. One of the loves of my life; God blessed me with him, then repeated that same joy with a daughter years later. Lord, these two young people complete me. I love them more than words could ever be put to paper. I long to see the great and wonderful things they both will do with their lives. Lord, please stand by these two young people and allow them to be a beacon of positive energy for you Lord first, then the community in which they live. In Jesus' name I pray, Amen!

The phone rings around 4:00 p.m. It's the courthouse. My minister, best friend, her sisters, the girlfriend, and brothers from the church all head to the courthouse.

"All Rise!"

About *Virginia A. Clark*

Virginia A. Clark is a writer, singer, structured hairstylist, and retired operations manager. This Virginia-born and reared native offers a revealing account of a graced career and turbulent span of life, charting the development of a persona that has made her one of America's vigilant, loving, and steadfast mothers. Through a never-before-told story from a particular point in her life, Virginia shares lessons about grit, determination, and a mother's love to free her son. One of her favorite scriptures is Luke 12:48: *"To whom much is given, much will be required."* Virginia is married, has two children, and three grandchildren with one on the way. She may be contacted by email at sinvasing@gmail.com.

IT'S TIME TO HOLD THE LINE!
Patricia D. Harris

If I could just stay right here, staring at the ocean from my third-floor hotel room balcony and remain in my own little world, just me and God, maybe it would be easier to hold the line. If I could interact with the "real world" here and there and literally just sit on the beach, watching the waves crash, I would be just fine. I believe I could learn how to live from my true center in God. I would recognize that He lives in the deepest depths of my being and in eternal union with my spirit. It is at this deep level that God's peace reigns continuously, and I want to be right there at all times!

See, I believe God when He says there is a gold mine of peace deep within me waiting to be tapped into. Delving into the riches of God's residing presence would be so much easier. Constantly living from my real center, where God's love has an eternal grip on me, would become as easy as taking candy from a baby! *That place...*

Queens, I don't know where you are in your journey God has you on, but I have a pretty good idea of the challenges you are facing as you fight every day to hold on to His word and His promises. See, I too faced many of those challenges, but the key is to always hold on, never to give in, don't run, and don't flee. Trust what God has placed in your spirit despite what may be going on around you. God didn't just call you; He chose you because He could trust you, not because He thought you would walk through this with no mistakes and that there wouldn't be days you wanted to give up—days where you didn't question His word, days where you didn't beat yourself up, and days where you didn't believe the lies of the enemy. He chose you despite all those things because He knew you would remain faithful to His calling and every time you stumbled and fell, you would get back up and would eventually create a space that only He could penetrate.

He knew you would make up in your mind that you would no longer do things your way but seek God for His will concerning your life. He knew you would gain the courage to ask Him to help you reveal and release those things that have kept you hostage for so long and prevented you from showing up the way God has called you to do—those things that kept you from allowing God to help restore the broken pieces of your life, so you would remain in position to be used by Him.

Queen, trust me, I know what it feels like to walk in your shoes. It is my prayer that you embrace the courage, confidence, and peace God has placed inside of you to take the shoes off and put on your war boots. Queen, it is war time; no time to punk out, no time to have a "woe is me" party—it is time to hold the line!

I pray that after reading the testimonies in this book, you know you aren't alone in this fight, that you have an entire army of queens who are in this battle with you. We had you in mind when we wrote our stories. We knew you were out there taking blow after blow from the enemy, feeling like you were about to lose this war, and God said, "Not so!" I have an army of queens who have accepted the calling to hold the line on your behalf and although you may have lost many battles, you will not lose the war!

Queen, where are you going? Why are you fleeing? Don't you know you were called to hold the line? You were created for this; you weren't only called, you were chosen—you're not runner up, not sloppy seconds but handpicked. God saw you when everyone looked right through you. He heard your silent cries when everyone else ignored your screams. Hold the line, queen. *You! Yes, you!* Don't move and don't retreat. He has prepared you just for this!

Together, we will **pause** and take a deep breath, **process** and put our minds at rest, **pray** knowing God will hear our cry, and **proceed** in faith, thanking God for His mercy and grace!

About *Patricia D. Harris*

Patty Harris offers over 25+ years of administrative and planning experience, serving in various roles including Sales Manager, Chief Administrative Officer and Executive Assistant and more recently, Human Resources. In March 2014, Patty was recognized by NABFEME's as one of Delaware's Women Trailblazers, and in June 2015, she was recognized as a "Mirror" recipient with The Hilton, one of the highest honors given by Meyer & Jabara Management. Patty is the founder of Patricia D. Harris ~ Hospitality Brokerage Firm, an event planning business, co-owner of Out of the Ashes: Where A Seed Finds Life, where restoring families dealing with trauma stemming from incarceration is their primary focus, and the organizer of the Facebook Group "Black Mothers", where the vision for the first collaborative book project, "Hold the Line" was birthed! Patty has heart for our Black mothers' mental, physical, emotional, and spiritual wellbeing. It is her ongoing goal that as God continues to breathe on her, she continues to breathe on her Queen Sistahs! Patty can be reached by the following methods:

Facebook - Patty Glasco Harris
Facebook Group - Out of the Ashes or Black Mothers
Website - http://www.outoftheashesllc.com/

EPHESIANS 6:11-18

11 Put on the whole armour of God, that ye may be able to stand against the wiles of the devil.

12 For we wrestle not against flesh and blood, but against principalities, against powers, against the rulers of the darkness of this world, against spiritual wickedness in high places.

13 Wherefore take unto you the whole armour of God, that ye may be able to withstand in the evil day, and having done all, to stand.

14 Stand therefore, having your loins girt about with truth, and having on the breastplate of righteousness;

15 And your feet shod with the preparation of the gospel of peace;

16 Above all, taking the shield of faith, wherewith ye shall be able to quench all the fiery darts of the wicked.

17 And take the helmet of salvation, and the sword of the Spirit, which is the word of God:

18 Praying always with all prayer and supplication in the Spirit, and watching thereunto with all perseverance and supplication for all saints;

Made in the USA
Middletown, DE
10 June 2021